The Green Kingdom

The Green Kingdom

The 1972 Childcraft Annual

An Annual Supplement to
Childcraft—The How and Why Library

Field Enterprises Educational Corporation
Chicago London Rome Sydney Tokyo Toronto

Acknowledgments

The publishers of *Childcraft—The How and Why Library*
gratefully acknowledge the courtesy of the following
publishers, persons, and organizations for permission to
use copyrighted poems, excerpts from poems, and special
illustrations appearing in this volume. Full illustration
acknowledgments appear on pages 296–297.

"The Florist Shop," by Rachel Field. From *Taxis and
Toadstools* by Rachel Field, copyright 1926 by Doubleday &
Company, Inc. Reprinted by permission of the publisher
and World's Work Ltd.

"Four Seasons," by Rowena Bastin Bennett. Reprinted by
permission of the author.

"Green Fire," by Bliss Carman. Excerpt reprinted by
permission of Dodd, Mead & Company; by permission of
the Canadian publisher, McClelland & Stewart, Limited,
Toronto; and by special permission of the Bliss Carman
Trust, The University of New Brunswick, Canada.

"Indian Pipe and Moccasin Flower," by Arthur Guiterman,
from *The Light Guitar* by Arthur Guiterman, © 1923.
Published by Harper & Row, Publishers. Copyright renewed
1951 by Mrs. Vida Guiterman.

"Maytime Magic," by Mabel Watts. Reprinted by
permission of the author.

"Mists of Daybreak," by Yosa Buson. From *A Year of
Japanese Epigrams*, edited and translated by William N.
Porter and published by Oxford University Press.

"Night," by Sara Teasdale. Excerpt reprinted with
permission of The Macmillan Company from *Collected
Poems* by Sara Teasdale. Copyright 1930 by Sara Teasdale
Filsinger, renewed 1958 by Guaranty Trust Company of
New York, Executor.

"Package of Seeds," by Aileen Fisher. Reprinted from
I Wonder How, I Wonder Why, © 1962 by Aileen Fisher,
by permission of Abelard-Schuman, Ltd. All rights reserved.

"So This Is Autumn," by W. W. Watt, from *One Man's
Meter* by W. W. Watt. Copyright © 1959 by W. W. Watt.
Reprinted by permission of Holt, Rinehart and Winston, Inc.

"Tomato Time," by Myra Cohn Livingston. From *The Moon
and A Star*, © 1965 by Myra Cohn Livingston. Reprinted
by permission of Harcourt, Brace, Jovanovich, Inc.

Photograph from *Island Life* by Sherwin Carlquist,
© 1965 by Sherwin Carlquist. Reproduced by permission
of Doubleday & Company, Inc.

Preface

Take a trip into the Green Kingdom! Find plants that swim. Search for a plant that looks like a rock. Watch plants capture and "eat" insects. See a cannon-ball tree and a tree that was used for a jail. Discover why leaves change color and what plants do in the winter. And find out how you can have a garden no matter where you live.

Maybe you never think about plants. Most of us don't. We see them, smell them, and eat them. But we don't really pay attention to them. They are just "there." But plants are alive and active. In the Green Kingdom there is just as much excitement, struggle, and terror as in the Animal Kingdom.

For us, plants are the most important things in the world. One way or another, plants give us all our food. From plants we get paper, string, cloth, medicines, and a thousand other things. And, believe it or not, plants make all the oxygen we breathe. We couldn't live without plants!

Why, then, do we do so much to harm them? We pollute the air plants use. We pollute the soil from which they get many of the things they need to stay alive. We pollute the water in which many of them live. Find out what people who work with plants are doing to save them—and how you can help.

And, at the same time, discover the beauty that is all around you. Open your eyes and see—as never before—the wonderful, amazing, living things we call plants. Explore the Green Kingdom!

The Green Kingdom

Contents

Seasons of Life

Springtime is a green time
*   When seedlings start their growing.*
Summertime's a rainbow time
*   When many blooms are blowing.*
Autumntime's a brown time
*   When seeds are ripe for sowing;*
But wintertime's a white time
*   (It is the flowers' nighttime)*
When stars of frost are glowing.

FOUR SEASONS
Rowena Bastin Bennett

Sleeping life

It is the flowers' nighttime . . .

In many parts of the world it is winter, and the ground lies cold and hard beneath snow and frost. The sleeping trees are brown and bare. The dry, dead stems of last year's plants shiver in the cold wind.

But under the snow and in the frozen ground are millions of seeds, underground stems, and roots that will be next summer's plants. Each seed is a package of life, with a tiny plant and a store of food inside it. On the roots and stems are buds, and each bud is the heart of a sleeping plant. A little warmth, a taste of water, and the plants will awake again.

And down in the ground, or snuggled beneath the snow-covered leaves, summer animals—chipmunks, frogs, ants, spiders —are sleeping, too. Like the plants, the animals are also waiting for warmth and life to come back to the land.

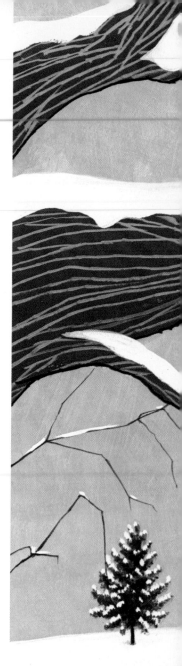

Wake-up time

The winter months slide slowly by. The sun begins to shine a little longer each day. The air grows a little warmer. The snow begins to melt and soak into the ground. The earth grows warm and wet and soft. This is what the plants have been waiting for.

Water soaks into the seeds. Their hard covers grow soft. The water makes the tiny plants and the stores of food inside the seeds swell up. The plants burst out of the seeds. From each seed, a tiny root pushes down into the earth, and a tiny stem with one or two leaves springs up.

The sleeping buds and roots of the older plants begin to stir. There is water in the ground again for them to find and drink.

Plants aren't the only things stirring. It is now wake-up time for many of the sleeping animals, too.

The world turns green

Now the tiny green heads of new plants are poking up from the brown earth and around the patches of snow. The little plants hold out their tiny leaves toward the sun. Their roots push down and spread out in the ground.

The roots of the older plants are working, too. They take in water. The water goes up through the plant and into the new little leaves.

The land is turning green, and green means food for many animals. So now the animals begin to appear.

Once again, plants and animals, the two kinds of living things, begin life anew in the springtime.

A world full of life

The days grow longer. The air is warm and the ground is filled with water. The new plants are shooting up. They twist and turn and stretch as they grow. They reach for as much sunlight as they can get. Their leaves grow to full size. Many of them have flowers. Many of the trees and other plants have flowers, too.

Animals of all kinds are everywhere. Many of them are laying eggs or having babies. It is the beginning of summer.

A butterfly and a buttercup

A butterfly belongs to the Animal Kingdom. A buttercup belongs to the Plant Kingdom. The butterfly moves through the air. The buttercup is rooted in the ground. They seem very different from each other. But are they?

Butterflies and most other animals come from eggs. And so do buttercups and most plants! A plant's egg is hidden inside a seed. The inside of a plant egg grows into a tiny plant and a store of food. The inside of a butterfly egg grows into a tiny, curled-up caterpillar and a store of food.

A caterpillar hatches from an egg and begins to eat. A buttercup sprouts from a seed and begins to make food for itself. Both the caterpillar and the buttercup must have food, water, and air to live. So must all plants and animals.

A caterpillar grows. So does a buttercup. The caterpillar changes into a brightly colored butterfly. The buttercup bursts out with bright little flowers. When these things happen, both the butterfly and the buttercup have reached an important part of their lives. The butterfly will mate and lay eggs. The buttercup flowers will grow seeds. The butterfly eggs will become new little caterpillars. And the buttercup seeds will become new little buttercup plants.

So a butterfly and a buttercup aren't so different after all. Plants and animals both have the same needs and they both do many of the same things. They are both living creatures, each with its own way of life.

Plants at work

During the warm summer months all the plants work to stay alive and to make new life. Their roots take in water. Their leaves make food. Their flowers make seeds.

As the seeds grow, the flower petals wither away and drop off. Soon, nothing is left of each flower but the little swelling where the seeds are growing.

As the warm days pass, the swellings begin to change. They become something different on each kind of plant. They become berries, or nuts, or other kinds of fruits. Inside the fruits are the seeds.

These seeds must now go traveling. Some will float through the air on leafy wings or silky parachutes. Others have spikes that catch hold of an animal's fur. Some will be dropped in far places by birds and animals that ate the fruits the seeds were in. In each seed a tiny new plant waits to begin its life next spring.

When the plants make their seeds, it's a good time for the animals. Many of the seeds and berries and pods and fruits are good to eat. The animals that sleep during winter can now fatten up for their long nap. Others can fill their underground houses with food for the winter.

Settling down to sleep

By the end of summer the plants have done their work. They have made their seeds and sent them out to find new growing places.

For many plants, life is now over. But the trees and other plants that have longer lives are getting ready for winter. They have dropped all their leaves. The ground is growing cold and hard. Soon there will be no water for roots to find. Once again they must sleep until spring arrives.

The animals, too, are getting ready for winter. Many of the birds and insects have flown away to warmer places. Many of the animals that have stayed behind have already gone to sleep.

The green earth is turning brown. In a few weeks, snowflakes will come spinning out of the sky. The land will turn white.

It is the flowers' nighttime . . .

Plant Ways

Have you ever wondered why leaves change color in the fall? Or why some flowers smell nice and some don't? Or what pine cones are for? Do you know why some trees stay green all winter? Why tree bark is rough? What flowers do?

The next few pages answer questions you may have asked about plants. Some of the answers will surprise you!

Now far and near on field and hill
We watch the death of chlorophyll
As earl autumn rushes in
With xanthophyll and carotin.
I hold that ignorance is bliss
Considering the fact that this
Is how a botanist perceives
The colorings of autumn leaves.

So This Is Autumn
W. W. Watt

Why leaves are green

In the furry, finny, feathered world of the Animal Kingdom, there are many different colors. There are orange and brown giraffes, white polar bears, blue beetles, and red birds. But in the plant world—the Green Kingdom—the leaves of nearly all plants are just one color—green. Why?

The biggest difference between plants and animals is that animals eat and plants don't. Plants are able to make their own food. Leaves have a wonderful stuff inside them that makes food out of air and water, with the help of sunshine. This wonderful stuff is called chlorophyll. And chlorophyll is green.

So a leaf is green because it is filled with chlorophyll. And chlorophyll makes food for the plant.

Animals have no chlorophyll. They can't make food inside themselves as plants can. Neither can you. But wouldn't it be fun if you could? You would always be full and you'd never have to chew!

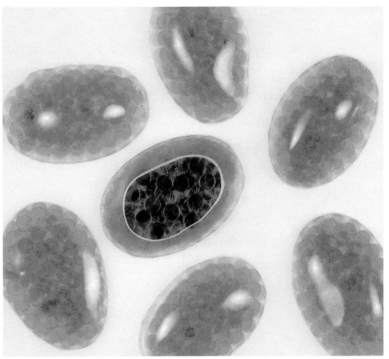

chlorophyll

Inside a leaf are millions of tiny
packages filled with green stuff called
chlorophyll. All these green packages
give the leaf its green color.

What leaves do

Leaves don't seem to do anything at all. But if you could become tiny enough to peek *inside* a leaf—you would have a surprise!

Sunlight comes into a leaf through the leaf's skin, which is clear like glass. Beneath the skin are millions of tiny "bags" called cells. These cells are like little balloons filled with water and living jelly. Inside the cells are small green packages called chloroplasts. The chloroplasts are green-colored because they are filled with a green stuff called chlorophyll. The chlorophyll catches some of the sunlight that falls on a leaf.

While the green packages are catching sunlight, other things are happening in the leaf. Air comes into the leaf through many tiny openings. Water, moving up from the roots far below, flows through the leaf. The air and water mix together and flow into the cells.

These cells are like little food factories. Here, the green chlorophyll works away. Using sunlight for energy, it changes water and a gas from the air (called carbon dioxide) into sugar. Some of this sugar is used as food for the plant. Some of it is mixed with minerals from the ground and is changed to other kinds of food.

So, all summer long, leaves are doing what leaves do best—making food.

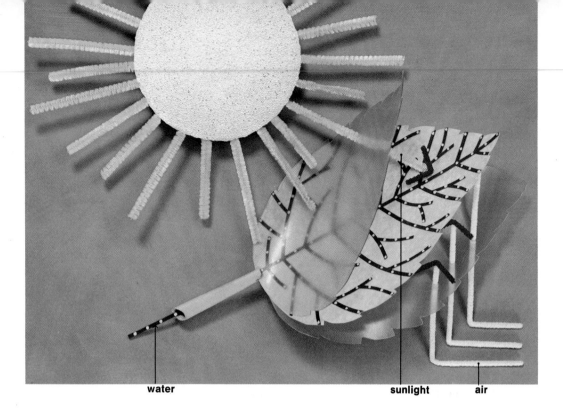

water   sunlight   air

Sunlight passes through the clear skin
of a leaf. Air comes in through tiny,
mouthlike holes. Water enters through
tubes in the stem. Using sunlight for
power, chlorophyll in the leaf changes
air and water into food for the plant.

cells and chloroplasts

A leaf is made up of tiny "bags"
called cells. Inside the cells
are green packages called
chloroplasts, where food is made.

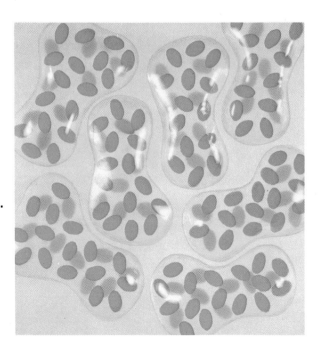

Why leaves change color in autumn

Inside a leaf there are millions of tiny packages of color—yellow, orange, and green. These colors have special names. The yellow is called xanthophyll, the orange is carotene, or carotin, and the green is chlorophyll. The green color covers up the others, and that's why leaves are green all summer.

Water comes into each leaf through tiny tubes in the leaf's stem. But near the end of summer, a thin layer of cork grows over the tubes and seals them up. No more water can get into the leaf. And without water, the green chlorophyll fades and disappears. Then the yellow xanthophyll and orange carotene can be seen. That's why many leaves turn yellow or orange in autumn.

All summer, leaves make sugar, which is a plant's food. Sap carries the sugar out of the leaf to other parts of the plant. But sometimes sugar gets trapped inside leaves when the tubes are sealed up. Then, the sugar may cause the sap to turn red or purple. And this makes the leaves look red or purple.

When leaves are dry and dead, they turn brown.

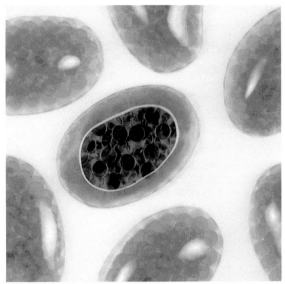

chloroplasts in summer

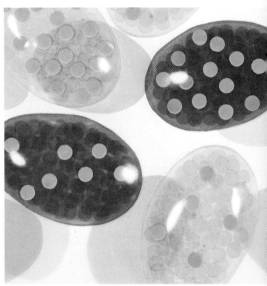

chloroplasts in autumn

Inside each leaf cell are tiny "packages" called chloroplasts. They are filled with colors. But, in summer, one color—green—covers up all the other colors.

In autumn, the green color in the chloroplasts slowly fades away. Then you can see the other colors. This is why leaves change color in autumn.

What roots do

Roots are like sponges. They soak up water. And roots are anchors, too.

A plant's roots grow down into the earth. They spread out and send out branches. They curve around stones. They grow toward damp places in search of water.

There is usually lots of water in the ground from rain that has soaked in. Mixed with the water are iron, copper, and other minerals. Plants need minerals to

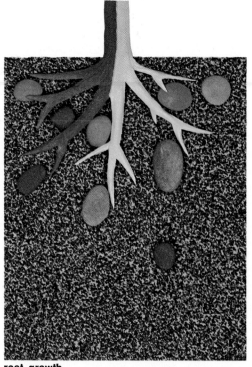
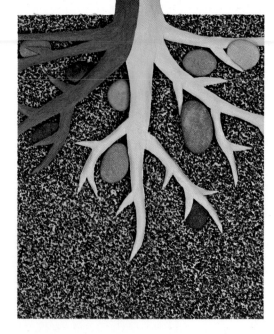

root growth

A plant's roots grow down into the earth. They send out branches that spread out and curve around stones.

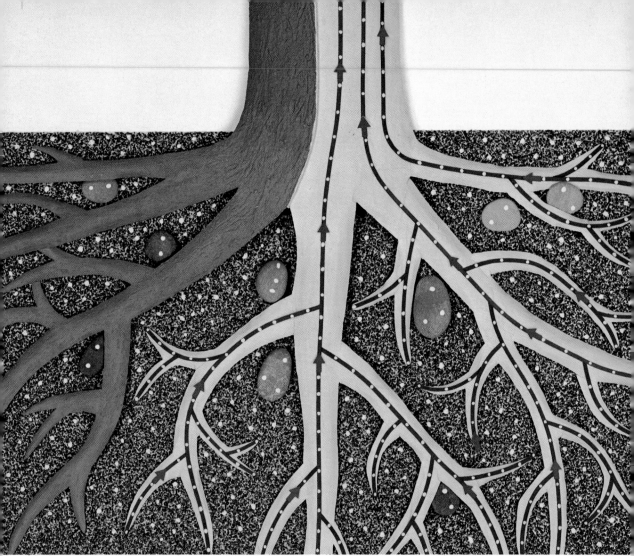

roots taking in water

Roots take water (dots) from the soil.
Arrows show water moving up the trunk.

stay healthy. Roots soak minerals up along with water,
and send them to all parts of the plant.

Besides getting what the plant needs from the soil,
roots do something else, too. By growing down and
spreading out in the ground, they hold a plant tightly
in place. Strong winds can't blow the plant away.
Floods of rain can't wash it away. It is held in place by
its root anchors.

Why some trees lose their leaves in autumn

Many trees that live where winters are freezing cold lose their leaves each fall.

Leaves make the food that keeps a tree alive. But to make food, and to stay alive themselves, leaves need water. A tree gets water from the ground. The roots take it in and the leaves pull it up through the trunk.

In late summer, a thin layer of cork grows where each leaf's stem is attached to the twig. Water can no longer get into the leaves. They dry up and die.

In summer, a tree's roots take water (dots) from the soil. The red arrows show how water moves up the tree, into the leaves. Some goes out into the air.

Wind tears the dead leaves from the branches. There is no reason for a tree to keep its leaves in winter. There is no water for them. In winter, the water in the ground turns to ice. The roots can't take in this frozen water.

But in springtime, the ground warms up. The ice melts. Rain and melting snow fill the earth with water again. Then a tree's roots start taking in water and the tree grows new leaves.

In autumn, the tubes that bring water to the leaves close up. Without water the leaves die and fall. Water stays in the tree in winter, but doesn't move.

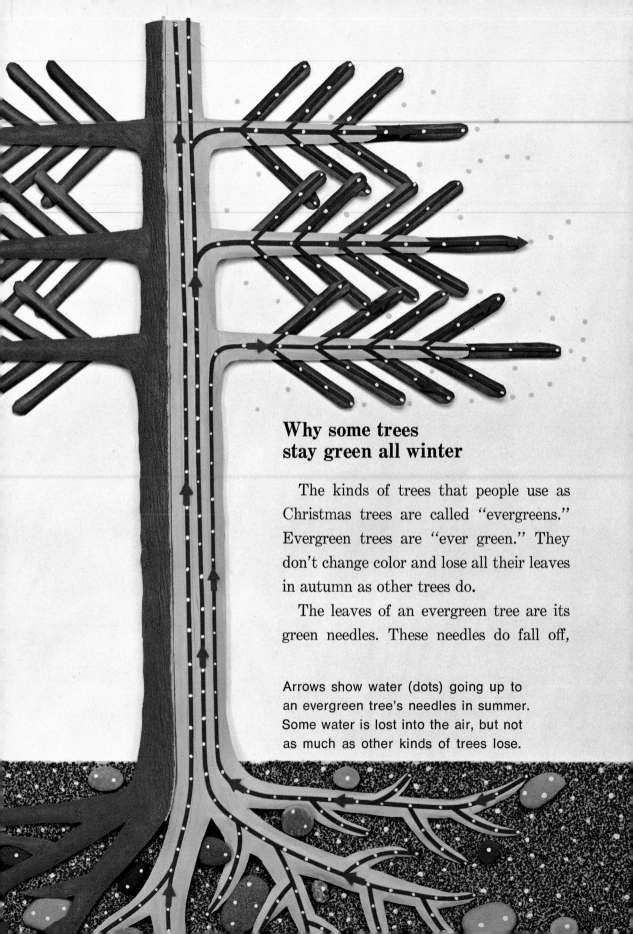

Why some trees
stay green all winter

The kinds of trees that people use as Christmas trees are called "evergreens." Evergreen trees are "ever green." They don't change color and lose all their leaves in autumn as other trees do.

The leaves of an evergreen tree are its green needles. These needles do fall off,

Arrows show water (dots) going up to an evergreen tree's needles in summer. Some water is lost into the air, but not as much as other kinds of trees lose.

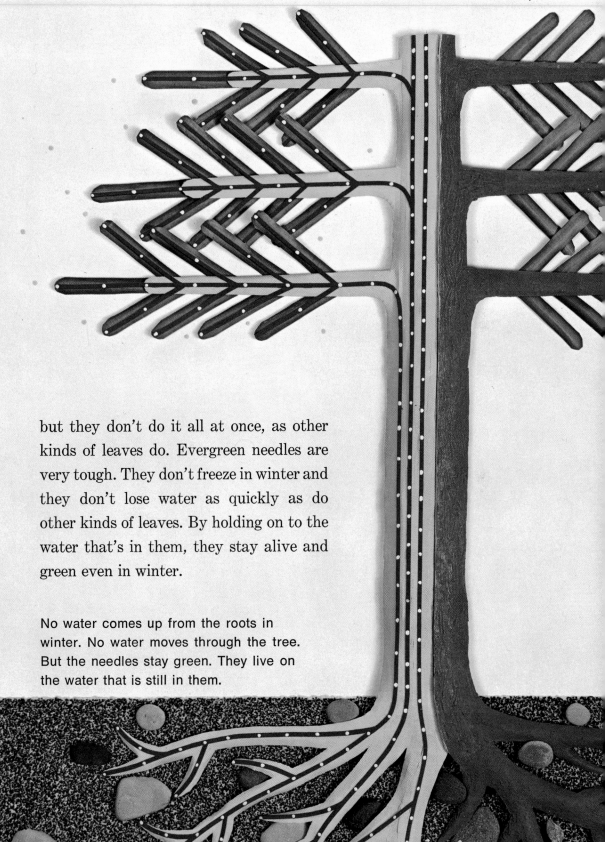

but they don't do it all at once, as other kinds of leaves do. Evergreen needles are very tough. They don't freeze in winter and they don't lose water as quickly as do other kinds of leaves. By holding on to the water that's in them, they stay alive and green even in winter.

No water comes up from the roots in winter. No water moves through the tree. But the needles stay green. They live on the water that is still in them.

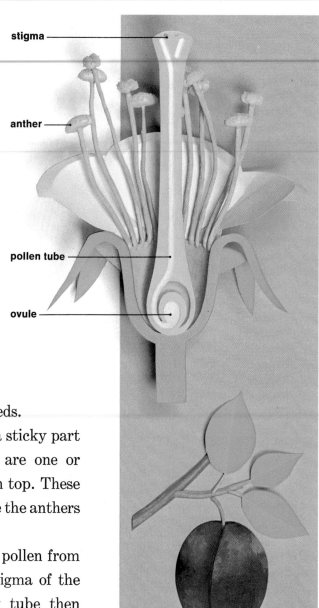

stigma

anther

pollen tube

ovule

how flowers make seeds

When pollen lands on a flower's stigma, a tube grows down to the ovule. Here it joins an egg to make a seed. The fruit forms around the seed.

What a flower does

A flower's job is to make seeds.

In the middle of a flower is a sticky part called the stigma. Around it are one or more tiny stems with knobs on top. These knobs are called anthers. Inside the anthers is a golden dust called pollen.

For a flower to make seeds, pollen from one flower must fall on the stigma of the same kind of flower. A tiny tube then grows out of the pollen. This pollen tube pushes down into a part of the flower called the ovule. Inside the ovule is a tiny egg.

The ovule now grows into a seed. Inside the seed, the egg becomes a tiny plant. The part of the flower where the seed grows becomes a fruit, with the seed in it.

How some insects help flowers

All flowers are seed makers. But to make seeds, a flower must get some pollen from another flower like itself. Many flowers need the help of bees or other insects to bring pollen to them.

How do flowers get insects to visit them? Well, flowers make a sweet juice called nectar, that many insects like. Flowers "advertise" the nectar they make. Their white or bright-colored petals and sweet scent tell insects that there is nectar for them.

Bees and other insects go to these flowers. To get the nectar, a bee pushes down into a flower. Sticky pollen from the flower's anthers falls on his body.

Then the bee buzzes to another flower and pushes down into it. Some of the pollen on his body brushes off onto a sticky part called a stigma. When this happens, the flower may begin to make seeds.

bee spreading pollen

Bees and other insects help flowers make seeds by carrying pollen from one flower to another.

salvia flower and bee

Flowers that are pollinated
by insects have bright
colors and sweet smells
to attract the insects.

Why some flowers smell nice— and some don't

Flowers that need the help of insects to make seeds have smells and bright colors. The smells and colors attract insects to the flowers. The insects carry pollen from one flower to another. The pollen makes seeds.

Most flowers have sweet smells that attract butterflies and bees and other insects that like sweet smells. Some plants, such as the skunk cabbage, have unpleasant smells to attract insects that like bad smells.

But some flowers don't need the help of insects. The pollen of these flowers is carried to other flowers by the wind. Since these flowers don't have to attract insects, they don't need bright colors or smells. They are usually small and greenish and grow in tight bunches. You can see such flowers on grass.

grass flowers

Flowers that are pollinated
by the wind don't need bright
colors or sweet smells.

What pine cones do

The pine tree is an evergreen tree with needles for leaves. It doesn't have flowers and fruits as trees with broad leaves do. The pine tree has pine cones.

Pine cones are seed makers.

There are two kinds of pine cones. One is small and papery. It is full of tiny grains of pollen that look like yellow powder. The wind blows the pollen out of the cones.

The other kind of cone is covered with wood scales. These look somewhat like the scales on a fish. At the bottom of each scale are two little egglike things called ovules. The wind brings pollen grains to the ovules. If a grain of pollen reaches an ovule, the ovule grows into a seed.

Each pine seed has a woody wing, and when the seed is ripe the wind blows it off the scale. When it reaches the ground, the seed may take root and grow into a new pine tree.

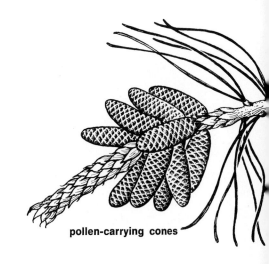

pollen-carrying cones

seed-carrying cone

insect galls on grape leaves

Why some leaves have bumps

Sometimes, the leaves or stems of plants become spotted with little greenish or yellowish-white bumps. These bumps are called insect galls. They are made when the eggs of an insect hatch out on very young stems or leaves. The baby insects cause a change in the growing plant. The change makes little swellings grow up around the baby insects.

Some galls look like beads, some look like marbles, some look like balls of pink cotton. The shape of a gall tells what kind of insect made it. The baby insect is protected by having the gall around it. And the baby insect uses the inside of the gall for food.

When insects lay eggs on leaves, little bumps called galls swell up all around the eggs.

insect gall cut open

The baby insects that hatch out of the eggs use the inside of the gall for food.

Why tree bark is rough

Bark is a tree's dead skin.

It is tough and hard and protects the soft, inside part of the tree.

A tree trunk grows from the inside out. Each year, a ring of new, soft wood grows around the trunk, inside the bark. This makes the trunk get thicker. The old, hard bark can't stretch as the tree gets thicker—it cracks, and splits, and crumbles away to powder to make room for the new wood. That's why a tree's bark always looks rough and cracked and bumpy.

As each ring of new wood grows, the outside of the ring becomes young bark. A tree is always making new bark and shedding its old bark.

Some trees, such as the beech, have smooth bark. These trees grow so slowly that their old bark isn't pushed apart and cracked. It just crumbles away to powder, a little at a time.

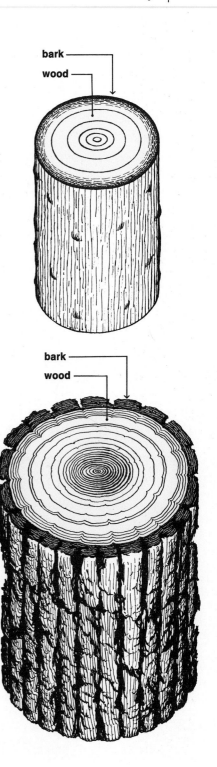

young and old bark

Tree bark grows from the inside. As new bark forms, old bark on the outside cracks and falls off.

Do plants ever move?

Plants are moving all the time. But they move so slowly we just don't notice these movements.

Instead of moving from one place to another, as animals do, plants move by growing. As a plant grows, it twists and stretches, turning its leaves to the light.

Some vines wind around a tree as they grow. Other vines, such as the grape or sweet pea, grow little arms called tendrils. These little arms reach out and wrap themselves around sticks or poles that people put nearby to help the vines grow.

Many flowers move their petals. They open them wide in the morning and close them tight at night. The leaves of some plants do this, too.

day lily

As the sun begins to rise, the day lily flower begins to open.

Moving very slowly, the day lily petals open.

Some plants have seeds and fruits that move. The witch hazel shoots its seeds out when they are ripe. The slim, dry fruit of porcupine grass has a long, sharp, twisted tail. In wet weather, when the ground is soft, the tail untwists and pushes the sharp, pointed fruit into the ground.

A jumping bean is a plant seed that seems to move by itself. But it doesn't, really. One kind of moth lays its eggs in the beans—one egg in each bean. The egg hatches into a little caterpillar that uses the inside of the bean for food. Sometimes the caterpillar hooks its legs into the bean and jerks its body as hard as it can. This is what makes the bean hop.

It has taken the day lily an hour and a half to open this much.

After about three hours, the day lily is all the way open.

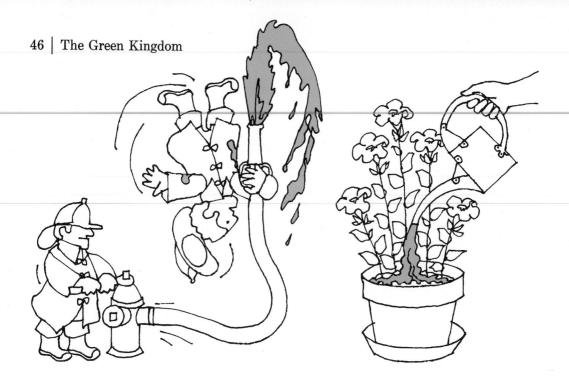

Why a plant wilts

Have you ever seen firemen using a fire hose? The hose looks stiff and fat while water is running through it. But when the fire is over and the firemen turn off the water, the empty hose is limp.

A plant is somewhat like a fire hose. As long as a plant's roots keep pumping water into it, the plant's stems and leaves stand up straight and stiff. But if the plant doesn't get enough water to stay filled, it will soon flop over, just like an empty fire hose.

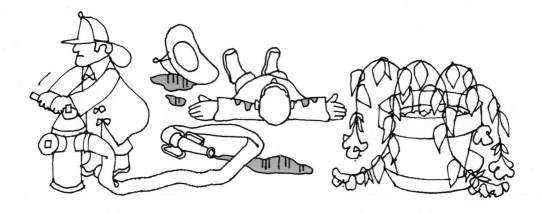

Can plants see, or hear, or feel?

A sunflower seems to watch the sun. It slowly turns its flower head as the sun moves across the sky. Can a sunflower see?

If you touch the leaves of a plant called the sensitive plant, they will suddenly fold up and droop. Then, in a short time, they will unfold and straighten up again. Can the sensitive plant feel?

Scientists say that no plant can really see or hear or feel. But plants *are* living creatures that twist and turn to move toward sunlight or away from heat. Most plants do this so slowly we don't notice it. But some plants, such as the sensitive plant, move quickly. This makes it seem as if they can feel. But plants don't have brains or nerves. So they probably can't feel pain the way you do.

sensitive plant

Before the leaves of the sensitive plant are touched, they are wide open.

When the sensitive plant is touched, its leaves suddenly fold up and droop.

Nature's Neighbors

Do you know that plants live in communities just as people do?

A forest is a plant community where many kinds of trees are neighbors. A pond is a community where many kinds of water plants are neighbors. Prairies, deserts, and even oceans are plant communities, too.

Plants live in places that have the kind of weather and soil they need. The plants in a swamp are there because they grow best in a wet, sunny place. The plants in a desert can get along well in a hot, dry place. Swamp plants and desert plants could never be neighbors.

Plant communities are called biomes. Every plant, animal, and person lives in some kind of community, or biome. If you wonder what kind you live in, you can find out from the next few pages.

Where the plants change their clothes

Do the trees where you live change their clothes during the year? Do they wear light green buds in the springtime, dark green leaves in the summer, and beautiful reds, golds, and purples in the fall? If they do, you live in the woodland community.

Trees—oaks, maples, elms, lindens, beeches, and many others—are the most important plants in the woodland. Once, these trees grew together in huge forests in many parts of the world. Most of these forests have been cut down. But if any of these kinds of trees grow near you, you're probably living where a great woodland forest once grew, long ago.

Most of the plants in the woodland grow leaves and flowers in spring and summer. These kinds of plants grow best where summers aren't too hot and winters aren't too cold, and where the ground receives just about the same amount of moisture all year round.

woodland community

Oak, maple, and hickory trees
are common in the woodland.

hepaticas

Plants of the woodland community

wake robin

black walnut tree

red oak tree

skunk cabbages

bloodroots

sugar maple tree

Life in the woodlands

In the woodland community there are four seasons.

In spring, little wild flowers are the first to bloom. Then trees and bushes bud. Birds appear and build nests. Soon the woodland is filled with squirrels, rabbits, and many other little animals.

In fall, the leaves change color. Most birds fly south for winter. Snakes, turtles, frogs, many insects, and some of the furry animals hibernate. But, if the winter is mild, birds, rabbits, and other animals stay active.

Giant lawns

Grass doesn't need as much water as trees and bushes do. So grass grows well in wide, flat places that are too dry for trees but not dry enough to be deserts. These places are like giant lawns. They are called grasslands or prairies.

The grass on a grassland may be short, middle-sized, or tall, depending on how much moisture there is. Hardly any trees

grassland community

Grasses and small plants with white or colored flowers are neighbors in a grassland.

or bushes grow on a grassland, but there are many small plants with white or colored flowers.

Big herds of sheep or cattle graze on many grasslands. Other grasslands have been turned into farmland where wheat and corn are raised. Wheat and corn grow well in a grassland because they themselves are grasses.

red top grass

Plants of the grassland community

pampas grass

rattlesnake grass

gray-headed coneflowers

Indian grass

purple prairie clover

Life in the grasslands

Most big animals that live on grasslands, such as zebras, eat grass. Most small animals, such as rabbits, eat plant leaves and seeds. There are also meat-eating animals—foxes, snakes, and, in some places, lions and leopards.

Many meat-eating birds, such as hawks, go hunting on grasslands. They swoop down to catch rabbits and other small animals.

It's hard for a hunted animal to hide on grasslands. The ground is low and flat and there are few trees or bushes. Many animals crouch down and hide. Some, such as rabbits and zebras can save themselves by running. And some, such as these prairie dogs, dig tunnels in which to hide.

Plants that like wet feet

Cats don't like wet feet. But the plants called cattails do. And so do many other kinds of plants. So these plants often live together in ponds, lakes, and rivers.

Cattails, bulrushes, and bur reeds live along the edges of streams and ponds, with their roots and parts of their stems under water. Water lilies and pondweeds live a little farther out, with their leaves and flowers floating on the water.

And some plants, such as the tiny duckweed, have no stems at all. They float on top of the water like little green rafts.

pond community

Cattails, bulrushes, and floating water lilies are often neighbors in a pond such as this.

water lilies

bulrushes

Plants of ponds, lakes, and rivers

lotuses

papyrus

arrowhead

duckweed

green algae

Life in ponds, lakes, and rivers

Plants that grow in and around ponds, lakes, and rivers give food and shelter to many animals.

Grebes and other water birds use these plants to make nests. Muskrats eat plants such as cattails and also use them for building houses. Frogs often fasten their eggs to water plants. And when the eggs hatch, the tadpoles use plants as food.

Bass and other big fish hide among the water plants. From these hiding places, they dart out to snap up careless frogs and small fish.

ocean community

Most ocean plants live in
shallow water where they
can get plenty of sunlight.

Underwater forests and meadows

Some plants live only in the salty water of the ocean. These plants live together in strange underwater forests and meadows.

Seaweeds live in shallow water near the shore, where they can get sunlight. They grow in great tangled bunches that hug the rocks to keep from being swept away by the crashing waves.

Eelgrass grows at the muddy bottom of shallow water along the edge of the shore. It looks like a lawn that needs mowing.

One of the strangest of all plants floats out in the middle of the ocean. It lives in a glassy shell that is a sort of box with a lid. This plant, called a diatom, is very tiny. There are billions and billions of them in the ocean. Diatoms are often called "the pasture of the sea." This is because these tiny ocean plants are the main food for many sea creatures.

a kelp forest

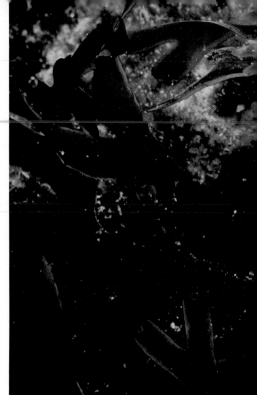

red-tongue seaweed

rockweed

Plants of the ocean community

corallina

sea lettuce

sargassum

Life in the ocean

Diatoms are tiny plants that live in the ocean. They can be seen only with a microscope.

Diatoms are green plants, and make their own food. Tiny, shrimplike copepods eat them. Small fish eat copepods. And the small fish are eaten by bigger fish.

Without diatoms to eat, the copepods would die. Soon, all the other sea animals would die. You can see how important the tiny diatoms are!

The Christmas trees' home

In the northern parts of the world, winters are long and cold and summers are cool. This is where many of the trees people use as Christmas trees live.

There are huge forests of spruce trees, fir trees, and other evergreen trees in the northlands. These trees like cold weather. In winter, they are covered with snow. Then, in spring, the snow melts and soaks into the ground. This gives the trees most of the water they need.

Evergreen trees and plants are able to live in many parts of the world. But the cold northern forest communities are the real "cities" of the evergreen trees.

northern forest community

◀ Most trees in the northern forest are conifers—trees that have cones.

twinflower

bunchberries

Plants of the northern forest community

birch tree

red pine tree

white spruce tree

Life in the northern forest

Evergreen trees grow close together in the northern forests. There are many ponds and lakes. Beavers, muskrats, moose, deer, and water birds live on the plants that grow around the water. Tigers once lived in the forests of Asia, but today the biggest cat in the northern forest is the lynx.

In the winter, it snows heavily. Many birds fly south. Squirrels and bears take long naps. Other animals, such as the elk, stay awake and active all winter.

Where trees take lots of baths

Many kinds of trees grow best where it is always hot and where they get lots of shower baths from the rain. These trees live together in forests in hot parts of the world where it rains heavily all year around. So much rain falls on these forests that they are called rain forests.

Rain forest trees stay green all the time. And they are much taller than most other kinds of trees. They are so tall they keep the sunlight from reaching the floor of the forest, so few plants can grow there. But many kinds of vines and plants, such as orchids, live high up on the branches of the tall trees. Here they can get sunlight. And many kinds of animals live in and under the trees of a rain forest community.

rain forest community

In a rain forest the trees are huge, and vines are as thick as a man's leg. Many people live in rain forests around the world.

stinkhorn fungus

Plants of the rain forest community

cannon-ball tree

bauhinia vine

passion flower

acanthus flower

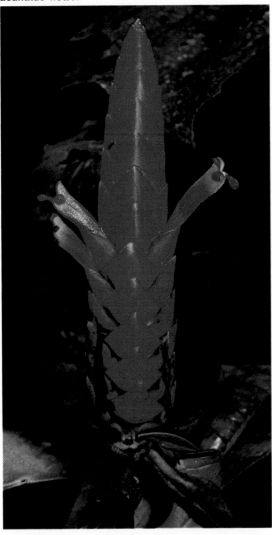

Life in the tropical rain forest

Life is always much the same in a rain forest. The trees are always green. It rains almost every day. The air is hot, night and day. Most animals live in the trees.

There are monkeys, tree snakes, and brightly colored birds. There are tree frogs and many kinds of tree-dwelling insects. And, in some rain forests, there are great apes such as the orang-utan.

desert community

Desert plants are able to live
without much water.

Plants that like it hot and dry

A desert seems like a bad place for plants. The ground is hard and dry, the sun is burning hot, and there's little water. Yet, many plants do live in deserts— plants that have solved the problems of living in a hot, waterless place.

Water is a desert plant's first problem. The only water most desert plants get is from rain. But it doesn't rain often in a desert. And when it does, the ground quickly dries. So, most desert plants have roots that spread far out and grow close to the top of the ground. These roots can catch lots of water, right away.

Most desert plants store up all the water they can get. Some plants, such as a barrel cactus, can swell up to hold a lot of water. Before a rain, a barrel cactus may look like a gray lump. But after a rain it looks like a fat, green ball!

Many animals might eat desert plants to get the water that's in them. But some plants have solved that problem, too. They are covered with thousands of sharp thorns or needles that keep animals away.

These thorns and needles also do another job. They cast shadows. A plant such as a cactus casts thousands of tiny shadows on itself. It makes its own shade!

beavertail cactus

yuccas

Welwitschia

pincushion cacti

Plants of the desert community

aloe

candelabra cactus

Joshua tree

Life in the desert

During the day, the desert looks lifeless. Most desert animals hide where they can escape the heat.

But when the sun goes down, a desert quickly cools. Little desert rats come out to look for seeds. Lizards hunt insects. Snakes hunt the rats and lizards.

It sometimes rains in a desert. When it does, the desert bursts into bloom, for there are many seeds in most deserts. But almost all of these plants quickly wither and die under the hot sun.

Plants of the frozen north

Far in the north, on the edge of the great sea that reaches to the North Pole, there is a great, flat plain called the tundra. Most of the time this plain is bare and frozen. The days are dark and sunless.

But, for a short time during the year, there are sunny days. The tundra warms up and the ice melts. Water soaks into the ground. And then plants bloom!

tundra community

The tundra is a great frozen plain, far in the north.

Even during these warmer, sunny days, a fierce, terrible wind blows over the tundra. So only tough, sturdy plants that grow close to the ground can live in this community. These include mosses, lichens, and small, flowering plants. Most of the tundra is a treeless plain, but sometimes there are birch and willow trees no bigger than bushes.

bilberries

Plants of the
tundra community

willows

reindeer moss

cottongrass

sorrel

Life on the tundra

In summer, the tundra is filled with animals. Little, mouselike lemmings and other animals eat leaves and seeds. And they, in turn, are hunted and eaten by animals such as foxes.

Winter comes suddenly. The ground freezes. Snow piles up. Most animals leave, but some stay. Lemmings burrow into the ground and live on seeds they stored away. Herds of musk oxen move from place to place, scraping with their hoofs to find lichens beneath the snow.

mountainside communities

Forest, grassland, tundra, and even
desert communities may all be found
on a mountainside.

Plant communities on mountains

A mountain is like a little world. It has many kinds of plant communities, just as the world has.

The upper part of a very high mountain is like the North Pole. It's always covered with ice and snow. The sun doesn't warm such high places very much.

But a little lower on a mountainside, the sun does give warmth. In summer, the sun melts the snow and many plants bloom. They're small plants that grow close to the ground. This keeps them from being ripped up by the fierce winds that howl around the tops of mountains.

A little farther down on a mountain is the tree line. That's the highest place where trees can grow on a mountain. Along the tree line, the trees are small and bent, and nearly all the same size.

Below the tree line, the trees grow taller and closer together. They make a big forest that covers the sides of a mountain. This part of a mountain is just like the northern parts of the world. It's cold and snowy in winter and cool and dry in summer. That's the kind of place where evergreen trees can grow, but other kinds of trees can't. So the forest is an evergreen forest.

Toward the lower part of a mountain it's warmer, and other kinds of trees can grow. If a mountain is in a part of the world where lots of rain falls, the lower part will be covered with a forest. But if a mountain stands in a place where not much rain falls, the lower part will be a grassy meadow. The lower parts of some mountains are even deserts.

Plants of mountainside communities

fire lilies

aspen tree

Engelmann spruce trees

buttercups

mountain gentian

edelweiss

Why tree-line trees are short

Every winter, snow covers the trees that grow near the tree line on mountains. The snow is about as deep one winter as the next.

When a tree is young, snow covers it each winter. But as it grows taller, the top will stick above the snow. Killed by the freezing winds that roar around the mountain, the top falls off.

In summer, the top grows again. In winter, it's killed. The tree can't grow taller than the deepest snow.

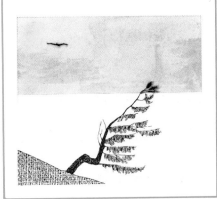

Strange and Surprising Plants

If you think that all plants are green, and have leaves, and grow in the ground, you're in for a surprise.

There are plants that are white, and orange, and even purple, instead of being green.

There are plants that grow on bread, cheese, rocks, and even in trees, instead of in the ground.

There are plants that look like animals and plants that look like rocks!

There is even a plant that looks like a ghost!

There are a great many kinds of the wonderful living things we call plants. And some of them are mighty strange and surprising!

mold growing on bread

When mold grows on bread,
it spoils the bread.

mold in Roquefort cheese

Some molds make the cheese
they grow in taste better.

Plants that grow on bread and cheese

When a piece of bread gets old, it may become covered with pale, powdery spots. Each spot is a sort of "forest" of tiny, tiny plants called molds.

Molds, like all living things, are made of many tiny packages of life. These are called cells. But it takes only one cell to start a whole forest of mold. This kind of cell is called a spore.

A mold spore is smaller than a speck of dust. It floats in the air. When it lands on bread or something else it can use as food, it begins to grow by sending out many tiny threads. Some of these threads grow down, like roots. Others grow upward,

mold growing on a dead moth

Molds that make dead things
rot, help make the soil richer.

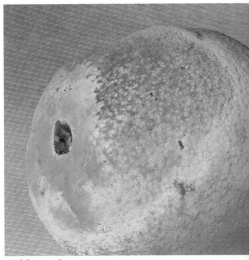

mold growing on an orange

When mold grows on fruits
or vegetables, it spoils them.

like stems. Bunches of these threads make
up the spots you see on moldy bread or
cheese.

Some molds spoil food. But others
make food taste better. Molds give such
cheeses as Roquefort and Stilton their
blue color and delicious flavor.

Molds grow on other things than bread
and cheese. Some molds grow on living
plants. This usually spoils the plant.

Some molds grow on dead plants and
animals. These molds help make dead
things rot and break apart. These molds
are helpful. They are part of nature's
clean-up crew.

mold on raspberry jam

Mold often spoils food in cans
or jars that have been opened.

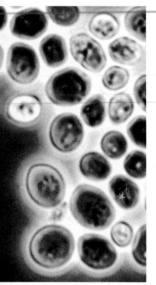

yeast plants

The baker's plant

If it weren't for a plant called yeast, we couldn't have the kind of bread we eat.

Yeast plants don't look like plants. They look like round drops of jelly. And they're so tiny you can see them only with a microscope. They float in the air everywhere. They don't do anything until they find a warm, wet place where there's just the right kind of food. And bread dough is just such a place.

Bread dough is made by mixing flour and water into a warm, wet paste. To this is added sugar, which is the yeast plants' favorite food. So when the yeast plants get into bread dough, things start happening!

Here's what happens. When a yeast plant takes in

yeast experiment

You need a package of yeast, a tablespoonful of sugar, ¼ cup of water, and a glass jar.

Pour the water into the glass jar. Now add the sugar and yeast. Mix everything together.

food it swells up and splits into two new plants! Then, each new plant takes in food, swells up, and splits in two! Soon, there are millions of new yeast plants!

As all these tiny plants take in sugar, they change part of it to a gas. This gas causes many little bubbles to form inside the dough. This makes the dough swell up. When the dough is baked, all the bubbles fill with air. Then the bread is light and airy. But without yeast to change the sugar into gas, the dough won't swell up.

Long ago, people let the dough sit in a warm place so that yeast plants would get into it. Today, bakers don't have to wait for this to happen. They buy yeast in packages and mix it into the dough.

As the yeast plants begin to use the sugar for food, the jar will fill with foam.

The yeast plants cause the foam by changing part of the sugar into a gas called carbon dioxide.

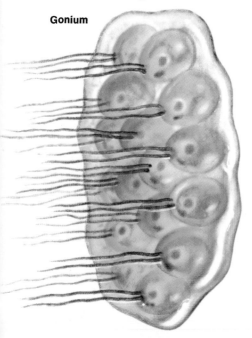

Chlamydomonas

Chlamydomonas is a tiny plant that swims like an animal!

Sometimes, 16 of these tiny plants form a jellylike wheel and live in it together.

Gonium

Plants that can swim!

If you peeked at a drop of pond water through a microscope, you'd be surprised! You would see many odd little creatures zipping about in the water.

One kind of creature looks like a green egg with two threads on one end. It has a red spot that's sort of an eye, for seeing light. And the creature swims by wiggling the threads. Is it an animal?

No, it's not an animal, even though it does move, as animals do. This green creature makes its own food, using sunlight, just as grass, trees, and other plants do. It's a plant—one of the plants we call algae.

Sometimes, 16 of these creatures fasten themselves together to make a sort of wheel. A kind of jellylike stuff holds them together. Each creature's two threads stick outside the wheel. When all the creatures wiggle their threads, the wheel rolls through the water!

And sometimes 32 of the creatures fasten themselves together into a ball. They keep their threads outside the ball and wiggle them to make the ball move, just like a bunch of men rowing a boat!

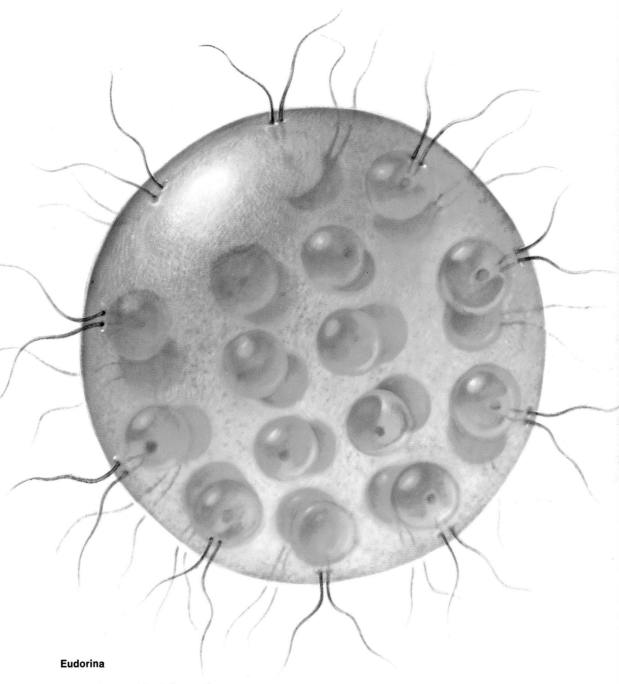

Eudorina

Sometimes, 32 of these tiny
plants form a jellylike ball
and live in it together.

A plant that acts like an animal

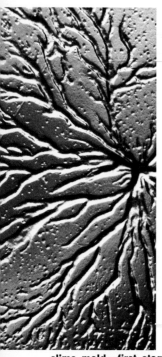

slime mold—first stage

This looks like frost on a window. But it is really thousands of tiny, living creatures, like drops of jelly. They are flowing together, just as drops of water do.

On a wet log in the woods, thousands of little creatures are moving. They are so tiny they can't be seen except with a microscope. Seen through a microscope, they look like shapeless blobs of jelly.

Suddenly the creatures begin to move toward each other. They cluster together. Soon there is a shape that's big enough to be seen without a microscope. It looks very much like a tiny, smooth worm. But actually it is made up of thousands of these tiny creatures, stuck together!

Now the wormlike thing begins to crawl. It moves very slowly along the log. After a while it stops. It begins to change. It changes into a long, thin stem with a knob on the end.

The knob dries, becoming hard and brittle. It breaks

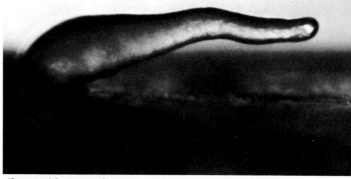

slime mold—second stage

When all the tiny creatures flow together, they form a shape that looks like a worm.

open. Out come thousands of spores—tiny living cells no bigger than specks of dust.

The spores float through the air. When some of them land on a wet log or pile of wet leaves, they change. They become like the tiny, shapeless blobs of jelly that turned into the wormlike thing. They begin to split in two, until there are more and more of them. Soon, they will begin to stream together to make another wormlike crawling thing!

The tiny, shapeless creatures, the wormlike thing, the knobbed stem, and the spores are all *one* living creature! It is called a slime mold. Some scientists say the slime mold is an animal. But because it comes from spores, as many plants do, it is usually thought of as a plant—a plant that acts like an animal!

slime mold—third stage

The wormlike shape crawls for a while. Then it stops crawling and begins to change once again.

slime mold—fourth stage

The wormlike thing becomes a plantlike thing—a stem with a knob on the end of it.

sundew

An aphid has been caught by the sticky hairs of the sundew plant.

Plants that trap insects

In many wet and swampy places there are plants that trap insects! But plants don't "eat." If plants don't "eat," then why do they catch insects?

All plants need a salt called a nitrate. It helps them grow. Most plants get this salt from the ground, but there isn't much of it in swamps. So some plants trap and digest insects to get the salt they need.

Plants that trap insects have different ways of catching them. The plant called a sundew has leaves that are covered with little hairs. On each hair there is a drop of sticky liquid. The sun sparkles on these drops and attracts insects. But when an

Venus's-flytrap

A careless lacewing walks into the open leaf of a Venus's-flytrap.

Like a big mouth, the leaf of the Venus's-flytrap begins to close.

insect touches one of the drops, it is stuck fast! Then, all the hairs around the insect bend over slowly. They push the insect down against the leaf. A juice oozes out of the leaf and slowly digests the insect!

The plant called a Venus's-flytrap works just like a trap. There are little hairs, like triggers, on each leaf. Around the edge of the leaf are little "claws." And each leaf can fold itself in half! When a fly or other insect lands on a leaf and touches one of the hair triggers, the leaf quickly folds in half. The little "claws" lock together and the insect is trapped. Then the plant digests it.

(continued on page 98)

The leaf is closed and the insect is trapped. Now the Venus's-flytrap will slowly digest the lacewing.

pitcher plant

Plants that trap insects

(continued from page 97)

The butterwort traps insects much the same way the sundew does. The butterwort's leaves are sticky. When an insect crawls on a leaf, it gets stuck. Then the edges of the leaf curl in. The insect is pushed to the middle of the leaf, where juice oozes out and digests it.

The pitcher plant drowns insects! Its leaves are shaped like vases. They are usually half-filled with rain water. Inside the leaves are little pockets filled with a sweet-smelling juice. An insect crawls into a leaf to get at the juice. But the sides of the plant are slippery and covered with hairs that point downward. The

A fly has fallen into the pitcher plant's leaf. The leaf is like a vase filled with water. The fly will drown and the plant will digest it.

insect slides down the hairs and falls into the water. It drowns and is digested.

There is even a plant that catches worms! It catches them with a lasso, just as a cowboy catches a cow!

This plant is a fungus. It grows under the ground and is so small it can be seen only with a microscope. It spreads through the ground like many tiny threads. There are many loops in these threads.

Tiny worms, no bigger than the threads, crawl through the soil. When a worm crawls through a loop, the loop suddenly tightens! The worm is caught! Then the fungus digests it.

A tiny worm crawls among the threads of a fungus. There are loops in the threads.

The worm crawls through a loop. Suddenly the loop tightens and the worm is caught!

fungus and worm

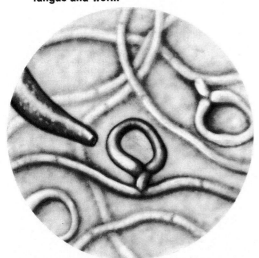

Green fur

Did you ever see a tree with green fur growing on it? If you rub this green stuff with your finger it even feels like fur. But it is really many thousands of tiny plants growing very close together. These plants are called moss.

A whole patch of moss can get started from just one tiny, dustlike spore floating in the air. When the spore comes down it puts out two tiny threads. One thread is like a root. The other thread sends out many branches, and from these branches the little plants shoot up.

Moss grows on trees, on rocks that have a thin cover of soil, and on damp, shady ground. When moss grows on the ground it looks as though someone had placed a velvety, green carpet on the earth.

moss

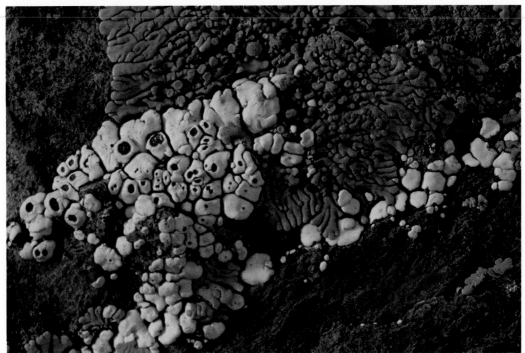

lichens growing on a rock

The rock-breaking plant

The plant called a lichen is full of surprises.

One surprise is that a lichen isn't just one plant. It's two plants that have become partners. One plant looks like a tiny bunch of tangled threads. The other plant can be seen only with a microscope. But one plant makes food and the other plant finds water. They share these with each other.

A second surprise is that a lichen doesn't have to grow in dirt, as most plants do. A lichen is able to grow on hard, bare rock!

A third surprise is that a lichen is able to break up rock and make soil out of it! A lichen makes a strong juice, called an acid, inside itself. It sends this acid out through many tiny hairs. The acid eats into the rock and slowly breaks it up into new dirt.

staghorn fern

Plants that live in trees

Do you know there are some kinds of plants that never grow in the ground? They grow high up in trees in tropical forests.

There's a good reason for this. In a forest where trees grow tall and close together, very little sunlight reaches the ground. The leaves block the sun. This makes it hard for other green plants to grow. They must have sunlight.

But orchids, Spanish moss, staghorn ferns, and many other plants get the sun they need by growing on the trunks and branches of trees. When it rains, their leaves and stems soak up and store water.

How do these plants get up into the trees? Most of them have light seeds that float in the wind. If one of these seeds is blown into a good spot in a tree it takes root. It spends the rest of its life there, hanging on.

wild pineapple

orchids

Spanish moss

Plants that climb

If a green plant doesn't get enough sunlight, it will die. The best way for a plant to get lots of sunlight is to grow tall. But if a plant with a very thin stem grows too tall, it will just topple over. So, as some plants grow toward the sun, they find things to lean on. These plants are called climbing plants.

A plant such as English ivy likes to be near a wall or tree. Then, as it grows, it has something to lean up against. Tiny roots grow out of the ivy's stem and stick to the wall or tree. These roots keep the ivy from falling down as it grows.

English ivy

honeysuckle

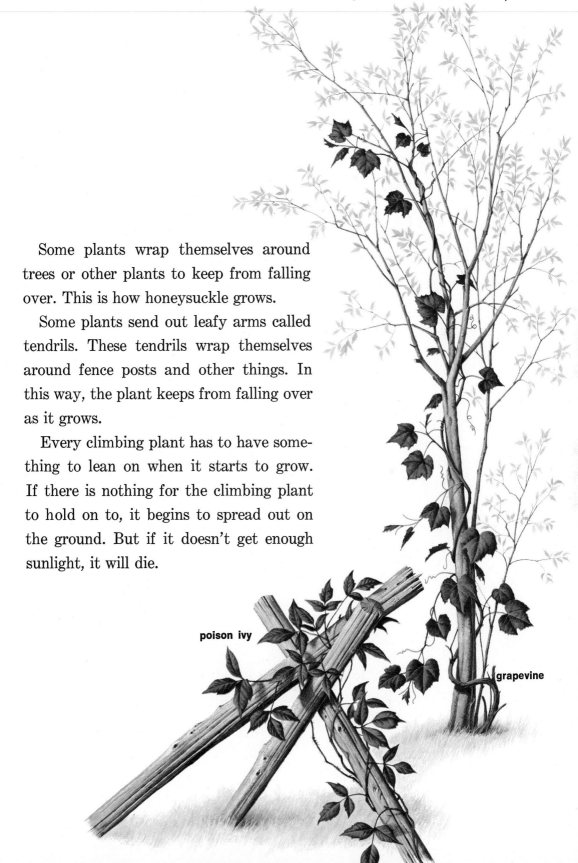

Some plants wrap themselves around trees or other plants to keep from falling over. This is how honeysuckle grows.

Some plants send out leafy arms called tendrils. These tendrils wrap themselves around fence posts and other things. In this way, the plant keeps from falling over as it grows.

Every climbing plant has to have something to lean on when it starts to grow. If there is nothing for the climbing plant to hold on to, it begins to spread out on the ground. But if it doesn't get enough sunlight, it will die.

poison ivy

grapevine

mistletoe

apple tree

Mistletoe is a vampire plant.
It often grows on apple trees.

Vampire plants

Some plants live like vampires.

They fasten themselves to other plants and suck food and water out of them!

When a plant called a dodder sprouts from the ground, it stretches out toward the nearest plant. The dodder's stem grows toward the other plant and slowly winds around it. The dodder pushes little threadlike roots into the other plant's stem. With these threads the dodder sucks food and water out of the other plant.

Finally, the dodder breaks loose from its own root. It spends the rest of its life wrapped around the other plant.

Mistletoe is a vampire plant, too. Mistletoe seeds are dropped on tree trunks by birds. The seeds send roots into the tree trunk. Then the mistletoe plant grows on the tree. The mistletoe can make some of its own food, but it gets all its water by sucking it out of the tree.

Indian paintbrush is a plant that seems to be minding its own business. But it's a vampire, too. Its roots spread through the ground and fasten to all the roots of other plants they can find. Then the Indian paintbrush sucks water and some food out of the roots of all its neighbors!

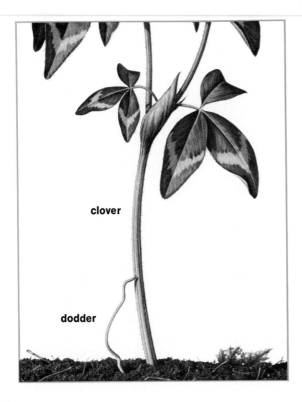

clover

dodder

When a young dodder sprouts,
it begins to grow toward
the nearest plant.

The dodder wraps itself around
the other plant. It gets its
food and water by sucking them
out of the other plant.

baobab "jail" tree

Odd and unusual trees

The world is full of unusual trees.

There's a tree with fruits that look like big sausages hanging from its branches.

There's a tree that looks like a giant umbrella.

There's a tree that looks like a peacock's tail.

And, in Australia, there's a tree with a hollow trunk that was once used as a jail!

traveler's palm

"dropsical" tree

sausage tree

rain tree

The biggest living things

The blue whale is the largest animal that has ever lived—bigger than an elephant, bigger than the biggest dinosaur. But even the blue whale isn't the largest living thing on earth. Trees are. And the largest of all trees are the redwoods and sequoias that grow in California.

The tallest trees in the world are the California redwoods. Most of them are more than 300 feet high—about as tall as a skyscraper with 30 floors! The tallest known redwood is almost 370 feet high!

One big sequoia is called the General Sherman tree, after a famous soldier. The tree is 272 feet high. The widest part of its trunk is more than 100 feet around and more than 36 feet across. A big crowd of people could hide behind this tree!

redwood trees

sequoia trees ▶

The ghost plant

Indian pipes

The plant called an Indian pipe looks like the kind of pipe Indians smoked. But it also looks like a ghost plant! Its flowers are white and its stem and leaves are white. It grows only in dark, shady places —like a ghost hiding in a haunted hollow.

Once, probably millions of years ago, the Indian pipe was green and could make its own food, like most other plants. But then it took on a partner. A fungus grew around the roots of the Indian pipe. The fungus got food from things in the soil and gave some of it to the Indian pipe.

Soon the Indian pipe was getting all its food from the fungus. Slowly it lost its green color. Now it can't make its own food. It can't live without its partner.

Indian pipe and moccasin flower
Grow where the woodland waves,
Grow in the moss and the bracken bower
Trod by the light-foot braves
Who played their part, who lived their hour
And left, with a name that thrills,
Indian pipe and moccasin flower
Scattered among our hills.

INDIAN PIPE AND MOCCASIN FLOWER
Arthur Guiterman

stone plants

The four brown rocks in the middle of
this picture aren't rocks—they're plants!

stone plants

Most of the time, stone plants
look just like stones. But after a
rain you can tell they are plants.
Tiny flowers pop up out of them.

Plants that look like rocks

In some deserts there are plants that
look like rocks!

Only the leaves of these plants show
above the ground. These leaves are fat,
covered with a tough skin, and are the
same color as the rocks and pebbles around
them. Because they are filled with water,
many desert animals would be glad to eat
them. But these leaves look like rocks,
so animals seldom notice them!

These strange plants are called stone
plants. The only time you can easily tell
that they are plants is after a rainstorm.
Then, a flower pops out from between the
leaves and blooms for a day or two.

The oldest living thing in the world

If trees had birthday parties, there's one tree in the world that would need more than 5,000 candles on its birthday cake!

Trees live much longer than people or animals do. A big oak tree, with a trunk so thick that you can't get your arms around it, may be hundreds of years old. The big redwood trees in California are thousands of years old.

But the oldest known tree lives on a mountain in the state of Nevada. It's a gnarled, twisted bristlecone pine tree. It's more than 5,000 years old—probably the oldest, living thing in the world!

bristlecone pine

cushion plant

The cushion plant

In New Zealand, there grows a plant that looks like a cushion made of white sheep's wool. It's called a cushion plant. And sometimes it's called a vegetable sheep.

A cushion plant is made up of thousands of tiny stems with millions of little leaves. The leaves are covered with tiny hairs, and that's what gives the plant its woolly look. The stems grow together so closely that they look like one big white lump.

You could even sit on a cushion plant if you wished. But you would be surprised. It isn't a bit soft—it's as hard as a rock!

young strangler fig

A bird drops a strangler fig seed on a tree branch. The seed sprouts. It sends long roots down toward the ground.

A plant murderer!

There's a tree that kills other trees to make room for itself. It's called the strangler fig. It lives in warm parts of the world.

Birds eat the fruit of full-grown strangler figs and drop the seeds on branches of other trees. If everything is just right, the seeds sprout.

A strangler fig seed sends down long roots. The roots creep toward the ground, winding around the other tree's trunk as they go. Soon the other tree is wrapped up in the roots of the strangler fig.

Once the strangler fig roots are in the ground they begin to grow bigger and stronger. They take more and more of the water, air, and sunshine the other tree needs. The other tree soon dies—murdered by the strangler fig.

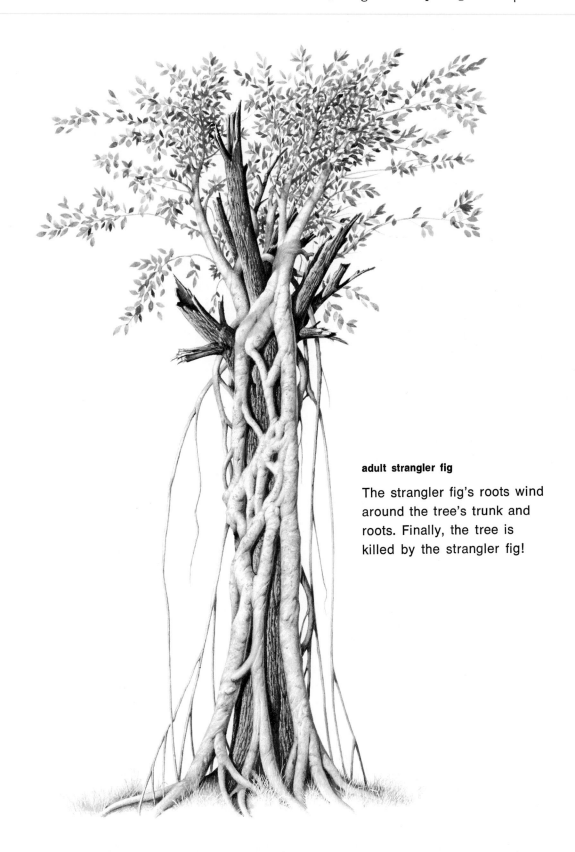

adult strangler fig

The strangler fig's roots wind around the tree's trunk and roots. Finally, the tree is killed by the strangler fig!

Weeds and Wild Flowers

Queen Anne's Lace in frilly white,
Dandelions gold,
Stalwart, seedy plantain spears:
These are weeds I'm told.

Though many folks may call them weeds
And weeds they well may be,
I stand and stand to look at them.
They're beautiful to me!

WEEDS
Leland B. Jacobs

The lion's tooth

Dandelions are good to eat!

For years, people in different parts of the world have eaten the young, spring leaves of dandelions. Some people boil them and eat them with salt and pepper. Some people use them in salads. These spring leaves are called dandelion greens.

The dandelion got its name in a funny way. The jagged edges of the dandelion's leaf look like a row of teeth. So, long ago, the people in France gave the plant the name *dent de lion,* which means lion's tooth. But to the people in England, *dent de lion* sounded like dandelion, and that's what they called this little plant!

There was a pretty dandelion
With lovely, fluffy hair,
That glistened in the sunshine
And in the summer air.
But oh! this pretty dandelion
Soon grew old and gray;
And, sad to tell! her charming hair
Blew many miles away.

DANDELION
Author Unknown

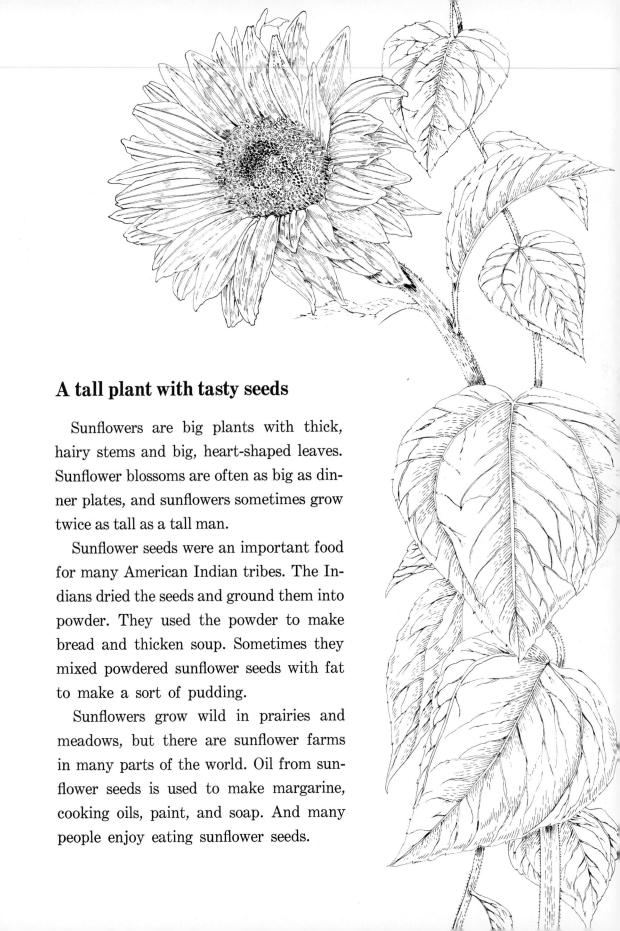

A tall plant with tasty seeds

Sunflowers are big plants with thick, hairy stems and big, heart-shaped leaves. Sunflower blossoms are often as big as dinner plates, and sunflowers sometimes grow twice as tall as a tall man.

Sunflower seeds were an important food for many American Indian tribes. The Indians dried the seeds and ground them into powder. They used the powder to make bread and thicken soup. Sometimes they mixed powdered sunflower seeds with fat to make a sort of pudding.

Sunflowers grow wild in prairies and meadows, but there are sunflower farms in many parts of the world. Oil from sunflower seeds is used to make margarine, cooking oils, paint, and soap. And many people enjoy eating sunflower seeds.

Jack-in-the-pulpit

Jack-in-the-pulpit

It's easy to see how this little plant got its name. It looks like a little man in a pulpit, ready to give a sermon. It's called Jack-in-the-pulpit because "Jack" is another word for a man or boy, just as "Jill" means a girl.

Jack-in-the-pulpit is sometimes called Indian turnip. That's because Indians used to eat the root, which looks somewhat like a turnip. The Indians didn't eat the roots raw, though. The roots have poison in them. The Indians let the roots dry in the sun for a long time. That got rid of the poison.

Jack-in-the-pulpit has a relative that grows in England and parts of Europe. It looks much like Jack-in-the-pulpit, but is called a cuckoopint.

Jack-in-the-Pulpit
Is preaching today.
What do you think
He is going to say?

I'm sure I know well
The message he'll bring:
Be glad for a green world!
Be glad it is spring!

JACK-IN-THE-PULPIT
Leland B. Jacobs

Arrowhead

If you were an Indian long ago, you might have gone wading to get some of your food!

Arrowhead is a plant with arrow-shaped leaves that grows in water near the edges of streams and ponds. When an Indian saw some of these plants, he might take off his moccasins and wade into the water. He would pull some of the plants out of the mud with his toes. Then he would boil the roots and eat them.

Arrowhead roots taste bitter when eaten raw. But when they are boiled they taste a lot like potatoes. Maybe that's why arrowhead is also called duck potato.

Indians liked to eat arrowhead roots. They pulled the plants out of the mud with their toes.

arrowhead

calamus

The perfume plant

Do you think it would be fun to have leaves on the floor of your house instead of a rug?

Long ago, people in Europe and early settlers in America would gather leaves of the calamus plant. They dried the leaves in the sun. Then they covered the floors of their houses with the leaves. The leaves had a nice, sweet smell that made a house smell good.

If you live near a pond, a stream, or a marsh, you might try drying some calamus leaves. Look for calamus—it is also called sweet flag—in shallow water. You'll know it by its long, swordlike leaves.

Long ago, people often gathered calamus leaves to put on the floors of their houses.

milkweed

A plant that bandages itself

There are lots of things to know about the plant called milkweed.

Milkweed gets its name from the white juice, which looks like milk, that oozes out when the plant is cut. This rubbery juice dries in the sun and covers the cut like a bandage.

Without milkweed plants, there might not be any beautiful monarch butterflies. Milkweed is the only plant on which female monarch butterflies will lay their eggs. That's because milkweed is the only food that monarch butterfly caterpillars will eat.

Milkweed seeds grow inside fat, green pods. In the fall, the pods turn brown, dry up, and split open. When the wind blows, the seeds are lifted out of the pod a few at a time. They have long, silky tufts, like parachutes, that carry them through the air on the wind.

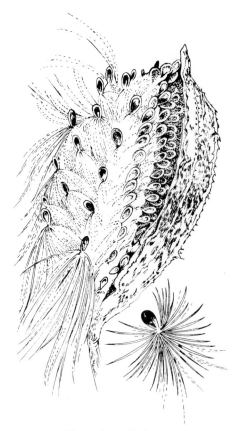

milkweed seeds in a pod

In a milkweed cradle,
Snug and warm,
Baby seeds are hiding,
Safe from harm.
Open wide the cradle,
Hold it high!
Come Mr. Wind,
Help them fly.

BABY SEEDS
Unknown

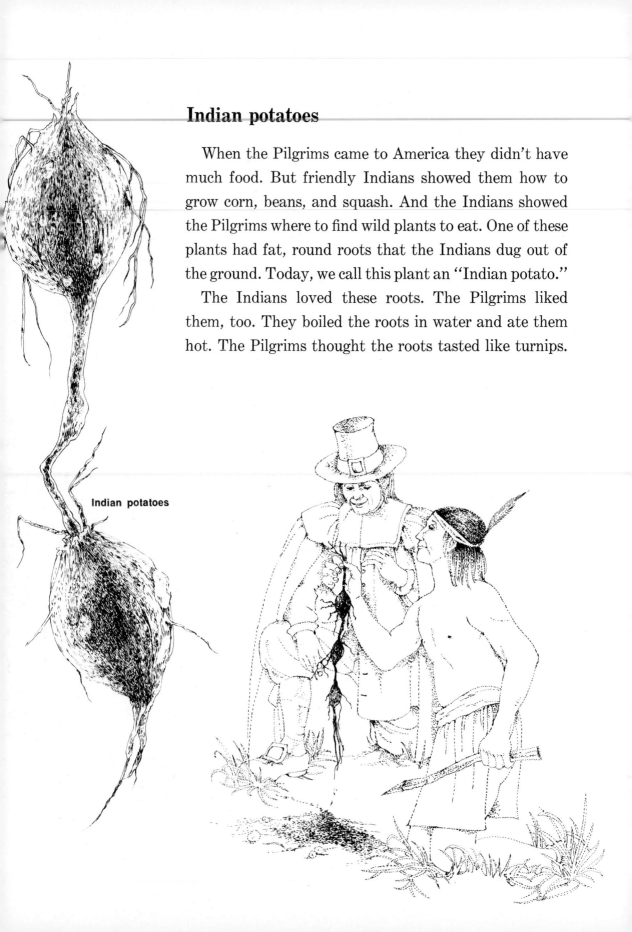

Indian potatoes

When the Pilgrims came to America they didn't have much food. But friendly Indians showed them how to grow corn, beans, and squash. And the Indians showed the Pilgrims where to find wild plants to eat. One of these plants had fat, round roots that the Indians dug out of the ground. Today, we call this plant an "Indian potato."

The Indians loved these roots. The Pilgrims liked them, too. They boiled the roots in water and ate them hot. The Pilgrims thought the roots tasted like turnips.

Indian potatoes

An Indian medicine plant

When you're sick, your mother calls a doctor.

Long ago, when an Indian child became sick, his mother called a medicine man. An Indian medicine man didn't have pills or shots to give sick children. But he could make many kinds of medicine from wild plants.

One plant the medicine man made medicine from was the May apple. With its slim stem and large green leaves, the May apple looks much like a little, green umbrella. It gets its name because its fruit—which really looks more like a lemon than an apple—appears in May.

The medicine man boiled the roots of the May apple plant in water. Then he used the water to help cure stomach aches. The pioneers in America learned about this medicine from the Indians. Then the pioneers used May apple medicine to cure their stomach aches, too.

May apples

Elves' umbrellas and toads' stools

Fungi are strange little plants. They have no roots, stems, or leaves. They look like umbrellas, or balls, or sponges, or horns, or even birds' nests! They are white, or yellow, or orange, or purple, or even polka-dotted—but seldom green. They usually grow in damp, dark places in woods, in piles of rotting leaves, or on old trees and logs. And sometimes they pop up on peoples' lawns.

The fungi you probably know best are the ones called mushrooms. They usually look like little umbrellas. In fact, people once believed that elves used mushrooms for umbrellas when it rained.

Mushrooms are often called toadstools. Someone with a sense of humor must have made up that name. But some mushrooms are just about the right size and shape to make a comfortable stool for a fat toad.

Some mushrooms are good to eat. But some are poisonous and can kill! Many people believe that poisonous mushrooms will turn a spoon or a coin black, or will make water turn black, but that's not true. There's no way to tell a good mushroom from a poisonous one unless you're an expert. So never eat a wild mushroom!

fly agaric mushrooms

morel mushrooms

bird's nest fungi

puffballs

club mushrooms

Fairies, sneezes, and piles of gold

Long ago, people in Ireland believed that ragweed was the favorite plant of the fairies. But it seems strange that the fairies would like a plant that makes many people sick.

In most flowers there are tiny grains called pollen. Ragweed pollen is like dust. It floats in the air. When it gets into people's noses, it causes a sickness called hay fever. Hay fever makes your eyes itchy and red. It makes your nose run. But most of all, it makes you sneeze.

The plant called goldenrod is often blamed for making people sneeze, too. But this is a mistake. Goldenrod pollen doesn't float in the air. It's heavy and sticky.

Goldenrod gets its name because it looks like a slim, green rod with a mass of gold at its tip. Its golden flowers bloom from late summer through autumn. They look like piles of gold along the sides of roads and in meadows.

ragweed

goldenrod

The day's eye and a cup of butter

Did you ever wonder how some wild flowers got their names?

The daisy looks somewhat like an eye. And, like an eye, it opens up at the beginning of each day. So, long ago in England, people named it "day's eye." In time, the name became daisy.

The buttercup got its name because it looks like a cup made of yellow butter. Long ago, people believed that butter was yellow because cows ate buttercups. But that's not true. Butter does get its color from what cows eat, but cows don't eat buttercups.

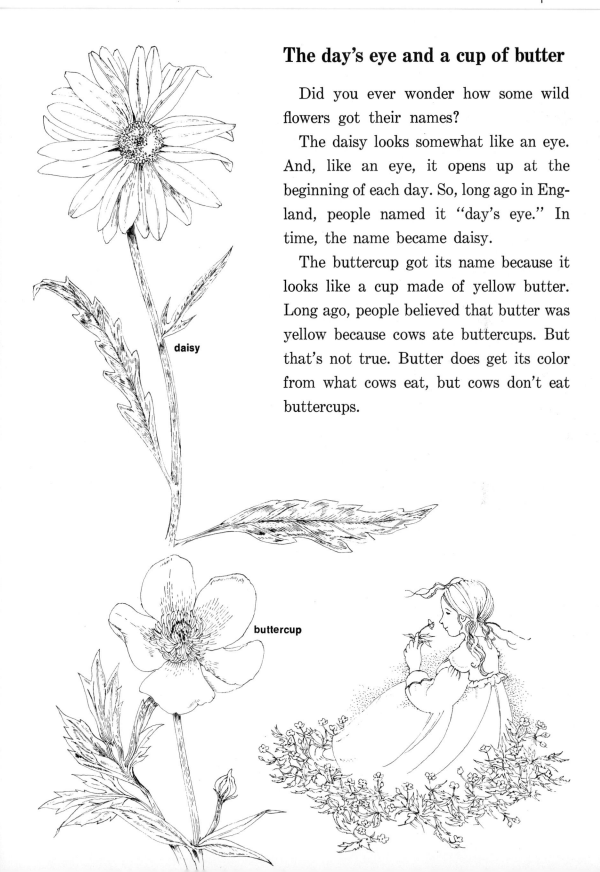

daisy

buttercup

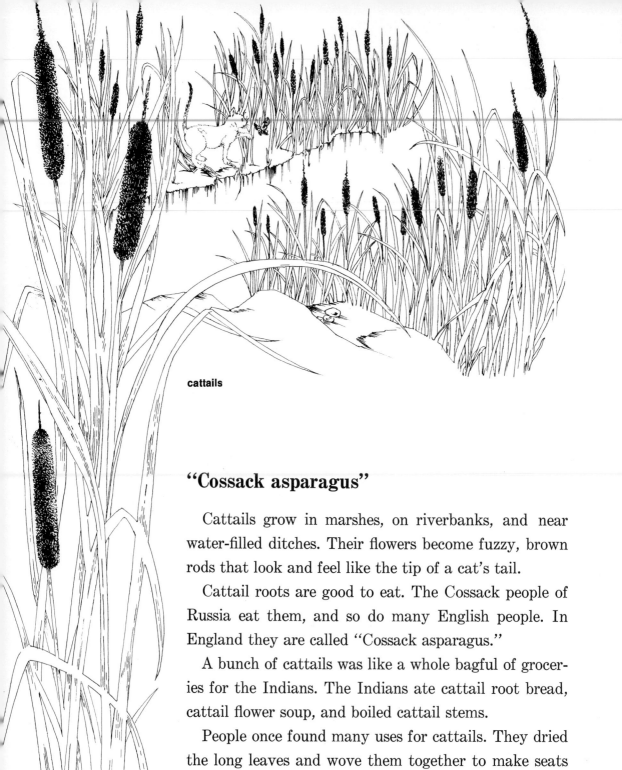

cattails

"Cossack asparagus"

Cattails grow in marshes, on riverbanks, and near water-filled ditches. Their flowers become fuzzy, brown rods that look and feel like the tip of a cat's tail.

Cattail roots are good to eat. The Cossack people of Russia eat them, and so do many English people. In England they are called "Cossack asparagus."

A bunch of cattails was like a whole bagful of groceries for the Indians. The Indians ate cattail root bread, cattail flower soup, and boiled cattail stems.

People once found many uses for cattails. They dried the long leaves and wove them together to make seats for chairs. They stuffed mattresses with the soft, cottony down that comes from the brown rods. And they used cattails for decorations, as many people still do.

Pot-cleaning plants

When your mother cleans her pots and pans she probably uses a scratchy ball of steel wool. But long ago, people cleaned pots with plants called horsetails.

Horsetails are short, hollow-stemmed plants that grow in sandy places. They are also called rushes. They have a rough, sort of glassy covering on their stems. This is the same kind of stuff that makes sand scratchy. When the people of long ago scrubbed their pots with the scratchy horsetails, the pots got nice and shiny.

The word "scour" means to clean well. Because the horsetails did such a good cleaning job, people gave them the name "scouring rushes."

horsetails

Horsetails are also called scouring rushes. People used to scour (clean) pots with them.

staghorn sumac

The Indian lemonade plant

Sumac is a small tree or shrub with narrow, pointed leaves. It tells people when fall arrives. Its leaves are usually the first to change color. They become bright, glowing red.

Towards the end of summer, bunches of red berries grow on some kinds of sumac trees. The American Indians made a drink from those berries. They dried the berries, mashed them, and mixed them with water. This made a sour, cooling drink that looked and tasted somewhat like pink lemonade.

One kind of sumac has white berries that hang down instead of sticking up as the red berries do. The Indians stayed away from that kind of sumac. It is poisonous and makes skin burn and itch!

The carrot's lacy cousin

From May until late August you can see the white, lacy flowers of a plant called Queen Anne's lace nodding at you along roads and in fields. The plant is named after a real queen who ruled England hundreds of years ago. People wore lots of lace on their clothes at that time, especially kings and queens. The person who named the flower probably thought it looked like the lace on the queen's dresses.

Queen Anne's lace is also called wild carrot because it is related to the kind of carrot we eat. But Queen Anne's lace isn't good to eat.

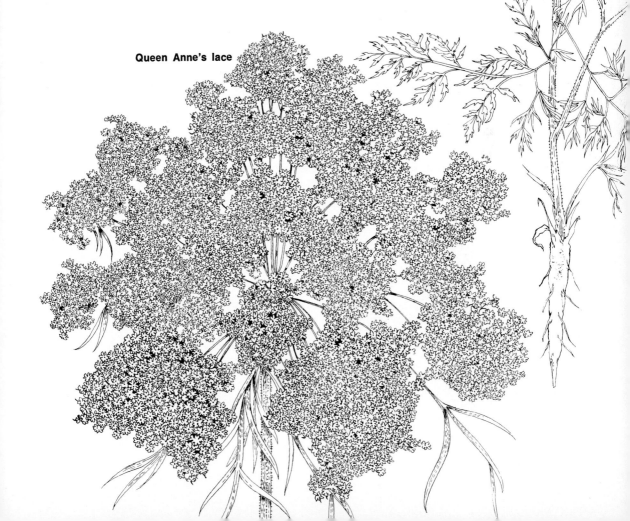

Queen Anne's lace

The plant that cats love

Cats just love the plant called catnip! A cat that finds a clump of catnip will happily roll about among the leaves. Many cat owners give their pets balls or toys made of dried catnip leaves. Many cats seem to like dried catnip leaves just as well as green, growing ones.

Some people like catnip, too—not to roll around in, but to drink. They make catnip tea by putting dried catnip leaves in boiling water and adding a little honey.

Catnip belongs to the mint family. It grows wild in many parts of North America and Europe. You can often find it along roads or near old farms.

When a cat finds a clump of catnip, it loves to roll over and over in the leaves.

catnip

A magic plant

Clover is a common plant. Its little red, white, pink, or yellow blossoms peep up from meadows and lawns everywhere.

Long ago, people believed that clover was a magic plant. They believed that three-leaf clovers would guard them from the spells of witches. They believed that four-leaf clovers would make them able to see fairies and elves. And, to this day, many people think that finding a four-leaf clover will bring them luck.

Of course clover isn't really a magic plant. But it does help make soil rich. And bees make fine honey from its blossoms.

clover

Deadly berries and seeds

Many kinds of berries and seeds look as if they are good to eat. But many are really poisonous! All the berries shown on this page are deadly, and can kill. So can castor beans, which are seeds. Never eat a berry, seed, or nut unless you know for sure that it is safe.

yew berries

deadly nightshade berries

castor beans
mistletoe berries

poison ivy

stinging nettle

Plants that make you itch and burn

The plants shown on this page can hurt you. If you should happen to touch one of them, it can make your skin burn and sting and itch. Learn to recognize these plants so you can stay away from them.

poison oak

Dangerous leaves

Some of the most beautiful and common plants have leaves and petals that can kill! Never chew the leaves, flowers, or branches of any plant!

oleander

The leaves and branches of the oleander are filled with poison.

rhubarb

We can eat the stems of the rhubarb plant. But its leaves will quickly bring death!

Cherries are good to eat. But the leaves and twigs of cherry trees contain a poison.

wild black cherry

mountain laurel

The leaves, twigs, and flowers
of the mountain laurel tree
can cause death.

Just one of the beautiful red
leaves of the poinsettia plant
can kill a child.

poinsettia

How Does Your Garden Grow?

They can't see their pictures,
they can't read the label—
the seeds in a package—
so how are they able
to know if they're daisies
or greens for the table?

It sounds like a fancy,
it sounds like a fable,
but you do the sowing,
the weeding, the hoeing,
and they'll do the knowing
of how to be growing.

PACKAGE OF SEEDS
Aileen Fisher

A window-sill garden

You can have a bright, cheerful garden in your house all winter—a window-sill garden of house plants!

You can buy small house plants at many stores. Put them on a window sill, or on a table near a window where there is plenty of sunlight. Keep the dirt damp, but not muddy. Flower pots have holes in them to let water seep out, so put a dish under each pot to catch the water.

Some plants may grow bigger. If so, move them to bigger pots. You can use tin cans or cottage cheese cartons. Have your mother or father put a few small holes in the bottoms of these homemade pots.

Plants such as ivy or philodendron look nice in glass bowls. But a glass bowl must have gravel at the bottom to catch the water that seeps out of the dirt.

geranium   chives   ivy

a window-sill garden

Not all plants will grow indoors. Those that will are called house plants. They grow well if they get plenty of sunlight. The dirt should be kept damp, not muddy.

coleus   **cactus**

avocado

Living-room gardens

Imagine having a tree or a vine growing in your living room! Many people do!

Rubber plants grow as trees in India. Philodendrons grow as vines in South America. But both make fine house plants in cooler parts of the world. They don't need much light—just a warm room, a little water, and a dusting from time to time. Mother-in-law's tongue is another good house plant.

sweet potato

mother-in-law's tongue

You can buy house plants in many stores. But you can grow house plants, too. Try growing a sweet potato. Stick four toothpicks into opposite sides of the potato. Then, put it in a glass partly filled with water. The toothpicks should sit on the rim, so that just the bottom of the potato is in the water. Put the glass in a warm room with plenty of light. You can do the same with an avocado seed.

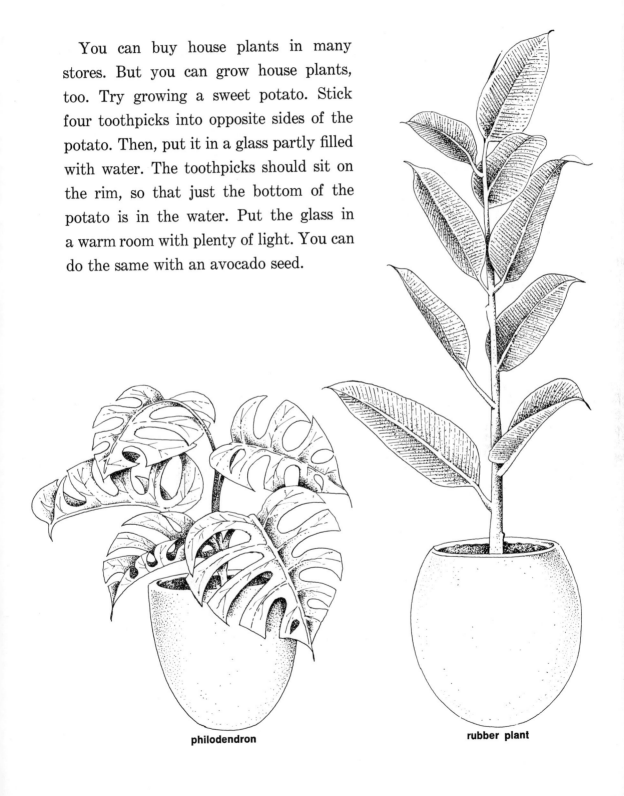

philodendron

rubber plant

Gardens in glass boxes

A terrarium is an indoor garden in a glass box. It's like having a tiny forest, all your own.

You can buy a terrarium, but it's more fun to make your own. You'll need a glass box, like a fish tank, or a large glass jar or bowl. Put a layer of pebbles on the bottom for water to drain into. Cover the pebbles with good soil, mixed with a little sand and peat moss. Water the soil until it is damp but not muddy.

Next, dig up some ferns, moss, and other small plants from a woods, meadow, or empty lot. If you want, you can also buy small terrarium plants. Arrange the plants to look like a tiny forest. Add small stones and twigs to make it look more realistic.

Keep your terrarium where there is light, but not where the sun will shine right on it. You can cover your terrarium, and temperature and moisture will stay in balance. But if the glass does get too moist, take the lid off for a short time.

An aquarium is a garden of water plants in a box. It's a kind of zoo, too, because it has fish as well as plants. But you will have to buy the fish and plants for your aquarium.

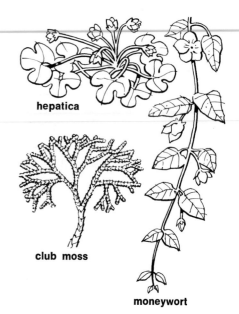

hepatica

club moss

moneywort

These are good plants to put into a terrarium.

These are some of the best plants for an aquarium.

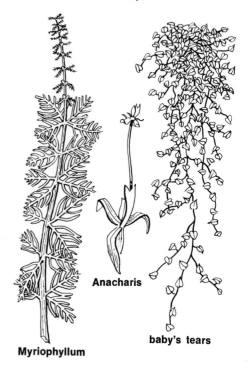

Myriophyllum

Anacharis

baby's tears

terrarium

aquarium

Outdoor gardens

A little seed
For me to sow . . .
A little earth
To make it grow . . .
A little hole,
A little pat . . .
A little wish,
And that is that.
A little sun,
A little shower . . .
A little while,
And then—a flower!

MAYTIME MAGIC
Mabel Watts

Planting an outdoor garden is truly fun! It's a thrill to watch little green heads come poking up from the places where you planted seeds!

All you need for an outdoor garden is a small patch of earth that gets plenty of sunshine. You can buy seeds for many kinds of outdoor plants. To plant them, just read the directions on the seed package.

The next few pages will show you some of the different kinds of outdoor gardens you might like to have.

a backyard garden

Wherever there's a little bit of
soil, there can be a garden. And a
garden brings beauty wherever it is.

rock garden

Rock gardens aren't very easy
to make. But they're fun, and
many people think they're the
most beautiful kind of garden.
Your rock garden won't have
to be as big as this one. But
it can be just as pretty if you
work hard at it.

A rock garden

If your yard has a sunny place that slopes a little, like a small hill, you can have a good rock garden. It should look like a tiny bit of mountainside where small, bright flowers grow among the rocks.

First, bring all your rocks to the slope. Put the biggest ones at the bottom. Scoop out shallow holes for them. At least half of each rock should be buried in the dirt.

Next, put the smaller stones higher up on the slope. Place some of them close together, but leave lots of dirt between others.

Finally, plant small ferns and flowering plants in the dirt between the rocks. Early spring is a good time to plant. Use plants that won't grow more than 12 inches high. Some good rock garden plants are shown on this page.

grape hyacinth

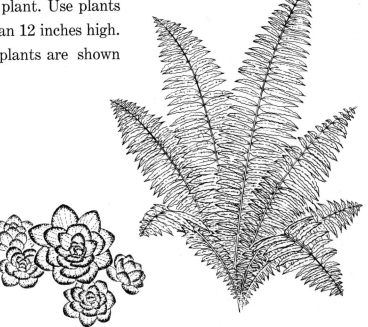

sweet alyssum

hen and chickens

ostrich plume fern

A vegetable garden

Nothing tastes quite so good as food you have grown yourself. To grow your own vegetables you will need a small bit of flat ground that gets *plenty* of sunshine.

It's easier to grow tomatoes from young plants than from seeds. Dig holes about two feet apart. Dig each hole deep enough to bury the plant's roots and wide enough to let them spread out. Fill the holes with water and let it soak in. When you put the plant in, the roots should rest at the bottom of the hole. Next to each plant put a four-foot high stick. As the plant grows, tie the stem to the stick to hold it up.

snap beans   carrots   radishes   lettuce

All the other vegetables shown on these pages—and many other vegetables—can be grown from seeds. Follow the directions on the packages. Water your vegetables only when there hasn't been much rain.

For more about the planning, planting, and care of a garden, look on pages 164–167.

On a summer vine, and low,
The fat tomatoes burst and grow;

A green, a pink, a yellow head,
Will soon be warm and shiny red;

And on a morning hot with sun,
I'll find and pick a ripened one.

Warm juice and seeds beneath the skin—
I'll shut my eyes when I bite in.

TOMATO TIME
Myra Cohn Livingston

cucumbers

tomatoes

Flowers you plant every spring

Most flowers that you plant in the spring are annuals. Annuals are plants that live only one summer. They sprout from seeds that are planted in the spring. In the summer, their flowers grow and make seeds. In the fall, the plants die. You must save their seeds, or buy new seeds, to plant again in the spring.

The plants shown on these two pages are annuals. Most of them grow from seeds. You can buy packages of flower seeds at many stores. But be sure you read the

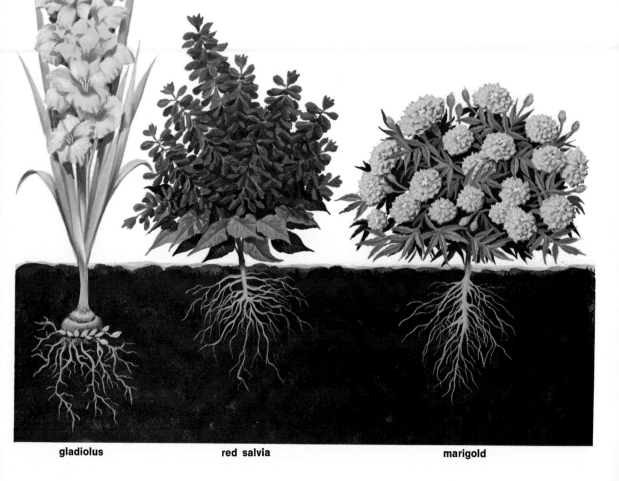

gladiolus   red salvia   marigold

instructions on the package before planting the seeds. In different parts of the world, spring comes at different times. The package will tell you when and how deep to plant the seeds.

Gladiolus plants are not really annuals, but where winters are cold we treat them like annuals. They grow from underground buds called corms. These corms are planted in the spring, like seeds. In autumn, they are dug up and stored in a cool place. Next spring, they can be planted again.

For more about the planning, planting, and care of a garden, look on pages 164–167.

zinnias

snapdragon

sweet peas

Flowers you plant only once

Some flowers don't have to be planted every year. You plant them just once, and leave them in the ground. From then on they bloom each spring.

Plants that bloom every year are called perennials. The plants shown on these two pages are some favorite perennials.

Lilies, tulips, crocuses, and irises grow from underground buds called bulbs or corms. You can buy bulbs at many stores. Most bulbs should be planted in the fall. But the package the bulbs come in will tell

delphinium   **tulips**   **iris**

you the best time to plant them. And remember, plant bulbs with their pointed ends sticking up.

Delphiniums and chrysanthemums grow from seeds, or from pieces of the stems of plants that are already growing. They should be planted in the spring.

Many perennials need protection during winter. The package your seeds or bulbs come in, or a gardening book you can get at the library, will tell you what to do for each kind.

For more about the planning, planting, and care of a garden, look on pages 164–167.

chrysanthemum   **crocus**   **lily**

A fun garden

All the plants shown on these two pages are "fun" plants. They have bright colors and unusual shapes. Several of them can be saved and used to decorate your house during winter or for special occasions.

Honesty and strawflowers are planted in early spring. Honesty blooms in May and June. The flowers become silvery seed pods that can be dried and put in a vase. Strawflowers bloom from midsummer until the first frost. They can be cut, dried, and used for decorations, too.

Gourds should also be planted in early spring. They ripen in the fall, growing into many shapes and sizes, with stripes and bright patterns. They will keep for years, and can be varnished or painted. Both gourds and Indian corn are often used as decorations for Halloween parties and Thanksgiving Day feasts.

Indian corn

flowering kale

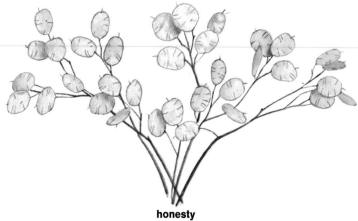

honesty

bells of Ireland

Chinese lanterns

gourds

strawflowers

Gardening tips

Before you can start your garden, you must pick a good place for it. Most garden plants need lots of sunshine, so choose a place the sun shines on most of the day.

Next, dig up the ground, turn it over, and rake it smooth. Your mother or father may have to help you do this.

When the ground is ready, mark off rows for the seeds or plants you're going to put in. Pound sturdy, pointed sticks into the ground. Then stretch twine between them as the children have done in the picture on the opposite page.

To make holes for seeds, push a pointed stick into the ground. If you're going to put in baby plants that are already growing, such as onions or tomatoes, you'll need a trowel. Use it like a big spoon, to scoop out holes.

To loosen soil, or dig up weeds, you can use a hand cultivator. Kneel down and pull it over the ground like a little rake.

Water the earth around each baby plant or seed until it is damp but not muddy.

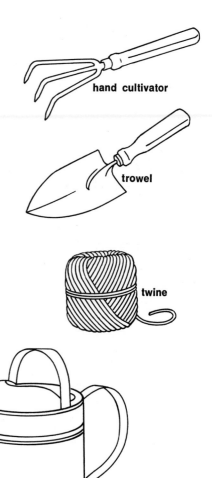

hand cultivator

trowel

twine

watering can

Spring Planting

This is how your garden might look when you start your spring planting. Each row of plants or seeds is marked off with string. The empty seed packages show what has been planted in each row. Most of the plants have been put where they will get plenty of sunshine. Many—but not all—growing plants need lots of sunshine. Some, like pansies, do well, or even better, in the shade. So these children have planted their pansies in the shade of the tree.

(Turn to next page)

Summer Weeding

By early summer, garden plants are usually well up—but so are the weeds! Here, the girl is pulling up weeds by hand, while the boy is using a hoe. He is looking at an insect that was eating one of his potato plants. He'll have to find a way to protect these plants from insects. The children will also have to water their garden if there is not much rain. If you have to water your garden, do it after the sun goes down. Then the sun won't dry up the water before it soaks in.

Autumn Harvesting

Harvest time is when the garden rewards you for all your hard work. Your flowers can be harvested as soon as they bloom. Picking garden flowers will help more to bloom. It's not so easy to tell when to pull up vegetables that grow in the ground. But the pictures on pages 156–157 will show you what some of these plants look like when they are ready for harvesting. And if you've planted any pumpkins, they'll be big and orange just in time for Halloween!

Famous Gardens

Many people have small gardens in their backyards. But there are many big gardens in the world, too.

A number of these big gardens are very famous. Some of them are really parks that go on for miles. Some are indoors, in buildings that were built especially for them.

These big gardens are useful. Often they are filled with plants from many parts of the world. This gives scientists a chance to study many kinds of plants without having to go to distant places. And it gives people a chance to see plants they might never see otherwise.

But, even more important, these big gardens are beautiful. They are a pleasure to see and pleasant to walk in. Many of them are so famous that people from all over the world come to visit them.

Indoor gardens

We usually think of gardens as being outdoor places. But many beautiful gardens are indoors, in special buildings. The plants get plenty of sunlight through glass roofs, and are kept warm all year long. So, even if there is snow on the ground outside, an indoor garden is always green and flowering.

Botanical Garden, Munich, Germany

Duke Gardens, Somerville, New Jersey

Longwood Gardens, Kennett Square, Pennsylvania

Chateau Garden, Villandry, France

Formal gardens

A formal garden is planted in careful designs. The flowers are arranged in squares, circles, or fancy shapes. Bushes are often trimmed to points, squares, or balls. Paths are long and straight.

Hampton Court Garden, Middlesex, England

Royal Gardens, Hannover, Germany

Natural gardens

Natural gardens are often called wild gardens because they look just like an ordinary woodland or meadow. But most of the plants in a natural garden are carefully planted by people.

A natural garden may cover many miles and may have lakes or streams or mountains in it.

National Botanic Garden, Kirstenbosch, South Africa

**Magnolia Gardens,
Charleston,
South Carolina**

**Strybing Arboretum,
San Francisco, California**

Favorite gardens

In every part of the world, people have a favorite kind of garden.

In Japan, people like gardens that have little bridges in them. In India, gardens often have ponds filled with water lilies. Gardens in Hawaii may have many ferns.

Gardeners in other parts of the world often copy these favorite gardens.

Foster Botanic Garden, Honolulu, Hawaii

**Daigo Temple Garden,
Kyoto, Japan**

**Botanic Garden,
Calcutta, India**

Mount Usher Garden, Ashford, Ireland

Meet the Trees

Can you tell an oak tree from a maple tree? Can you tell one kind of Christmas tree from another?

There are many different kinds of trees. But it's easy to tell one kind from another. Each kind of tree has leaves, bark, fruit, flowers, and seeds that are different from those of every other kind of tree. Some trees even have leaf-scar "faces" that help you tell them apart. And you can tell one kind of Christmas tree from another by the cones and needles.

On the next 15 pages is a game about trees. It's a game in which you follow a path through a spooky forest. If you take the wrong path you'll be in danger! But the trees will help you. If you can learn to tell one kind of tree from another, you'll always be on the right path.

So, come on—meet the trees!

The tree-path game

Come take a walk through this spooky forest. But be careful! If you choose a wrong path you'll be captured by giant spiders or eaten by crocodiles!

You can play this game by yourself. It begins here and ends on page 194. On all the game pages you'll find pictures of the forest, with many paths. You must take the right paths to get "home."

Each picture has a signboard that tells you what paths to take. Each path is marked by a picture of a leaf, or bark, or some other part of a tree. So, if the signboard says to take the "oak path," you must look for the path that has something from an oak tree next to it.

If you don't know much about trees, look at the tree identification chart below the picture. If you need to find an oak path, look for the oak tree on the chart. Under the oak tree are pictures of an oak tree's leaf, nut, flower, and bark. Look for the path that has a picture of one of these things next to it. It's the oak path.

If you take a wrong path, you'll know it when you turn the page. All wrong paths lead into danger. When you find you have taken a wrong path, turn back and try to find the right one.

TAKE THE APPLE PATH, THEN TAKE THE BASSWOOD PATH

Use this tree identification chart to find the right paths.

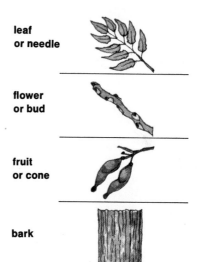

ailanthus

leaf or needle

flower or bud

fruit or cone

bark

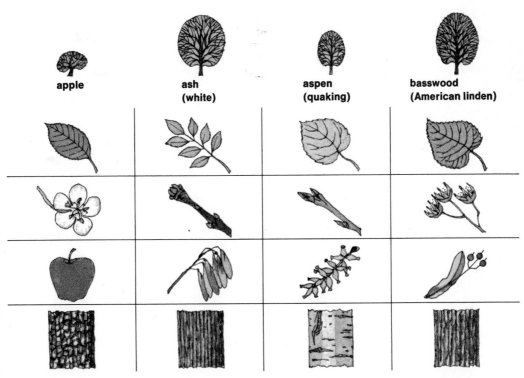

apple	ash (white)	aspen (quaking)	basswood (American linden)

Did you take the wrong path? Look at these clues to find your mistake.

 apple

 basswood

 apple

 ailanthus

 ash

 aspen

Use this tree identification chart to find the right paths. Start the game on page 180.

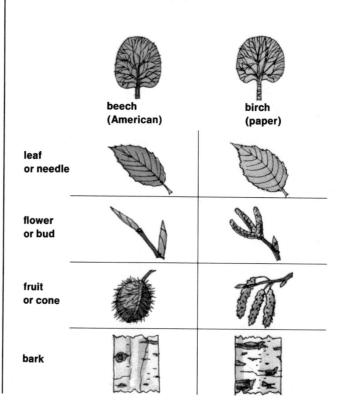

	beech (American)	birch (paper)
leaf or needle		
flower or bud		
fruit or cone		
bark		

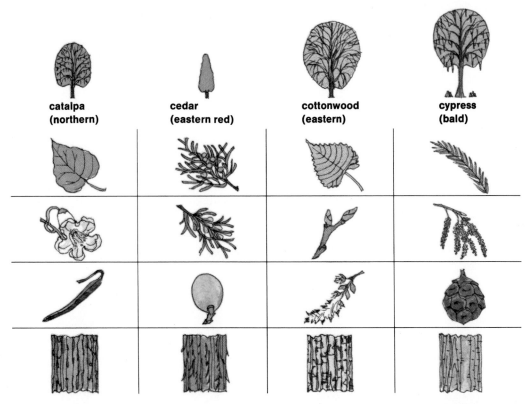

catalpa (northern)	cedar (eastern red)	cottonwood (eastern)	cypress (bald)

TAKE THE DOGWOOD PATH, THEN TAKE THE GINKGO PATH

Did you take the wrong path? Look at these clues to find your mistake.

 cottonwood

 catalpa

 birch

 beech

 cypress

 cedar

Use this tree identification chart to find the right paths. Start the game on page 180.

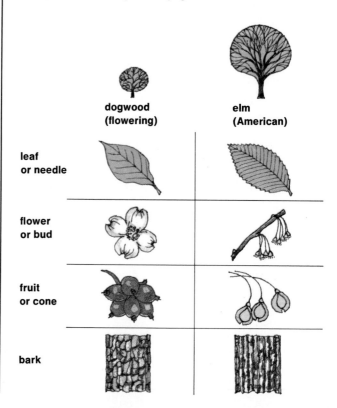

	dogwood (flowering)	elm (American)
leaf or needle		
flower or bud		
fruit or cone		
bark		

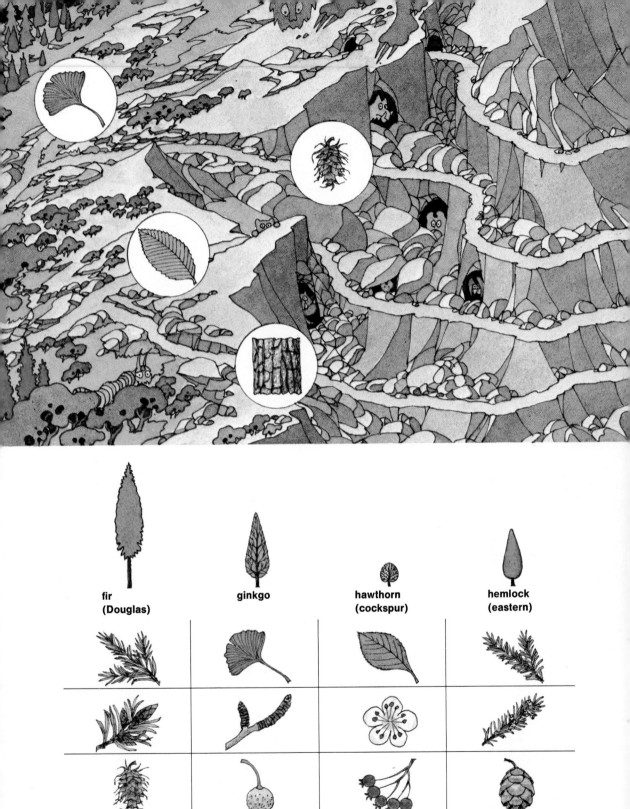

fir
(Douglas)

ginkgo

hawthorn
(cockspur)

hemlock
(eastern)

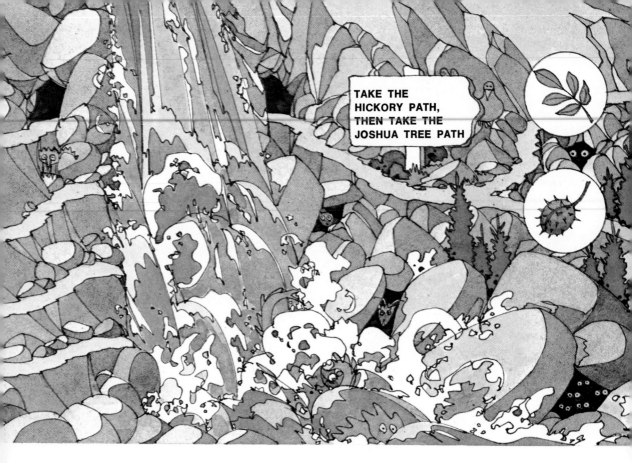

Did you take the wrong path? Look at these clues to find your mistake.

 dogwood

 ginkgo

 fir

 elm

 hemlock

 hawthorn

Use this tree identification chart to find the right paths. Start the game on page 180.

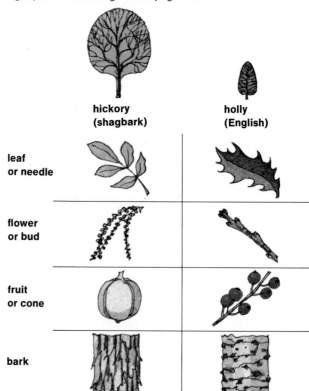

	hickory (shagbark)	holly (English)
leaf or needle		
flower or bud		
fruit or cone		
bark		

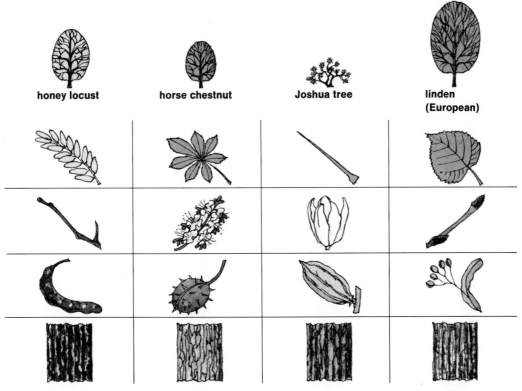

honey locust	horse chestnut	Joshua tree	linden (European)

TAKE THE MAGNOLIA PATH, THEN TAKE THE PALM PATH

Did you take the wrong path? Look at these clues to find your mistake.

 hickory

 Joshua tree

 horse chestnut

 holly

 honey locust

 linden

Use this tree identification chart to find the right paths. Start the game on page 180.

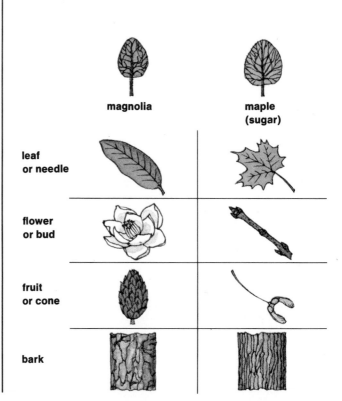

	magnolia	maple (sugar)
leaf or needle		
flower or bud		
fruit or cone		
bark		

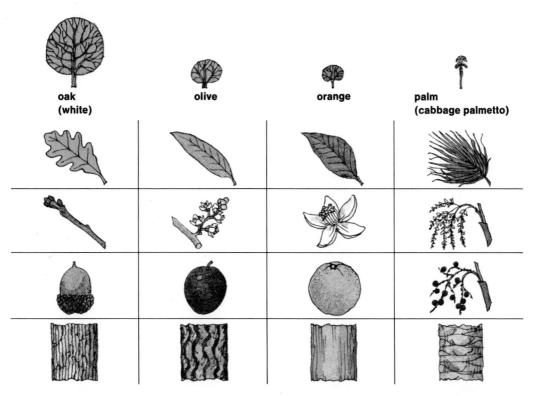

oak (white)	olive	orange	palm (cabbage palmetto)

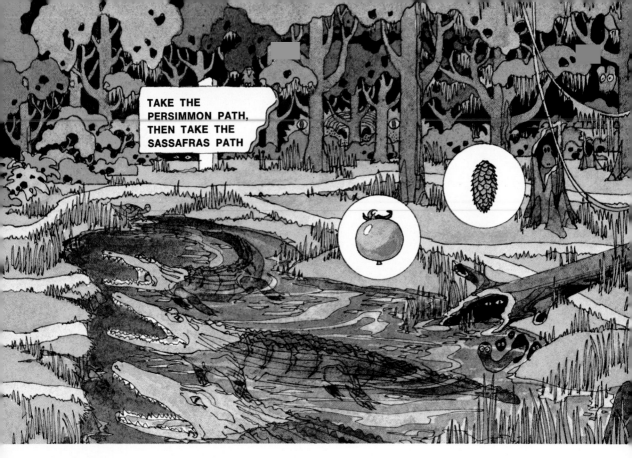

Did you take the wrong path? Look at these clues to find your mistake.

 magnolia

 olive

 oak

 orange

 palm

 maple

Use this tree identification chart to find the right paths. Start the game on page 180.

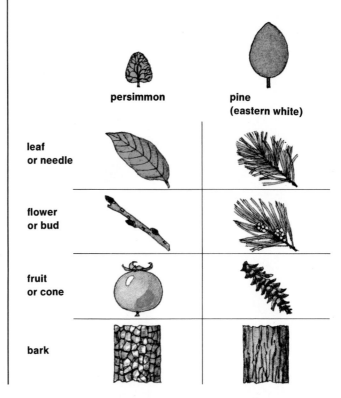

	persimmon	pine (eastern white)
leaf or needle		
flower or bud		
fruit or cone		
bark		

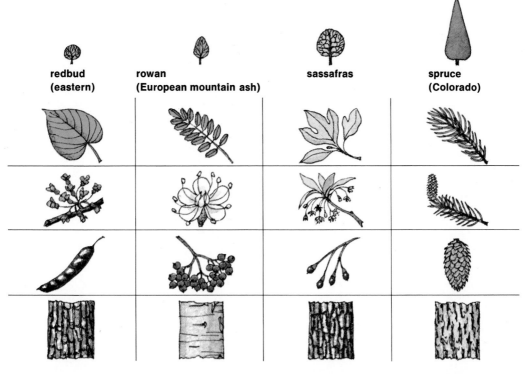

redbud (eastern)	rowan (European mountain ash)	sassafras	spruce (Colorado)

TAKE THE
SWEET GUM PATH,
THEN TAKE THE
WILLOW PATH

Did you take the wrong path? Look at these clues to find your mistake.

 persimmon

 spruce

 sassafras

 pine

 rowan

 redbud

Use this tree identification chart to find the right paths. Start the game on page 180.

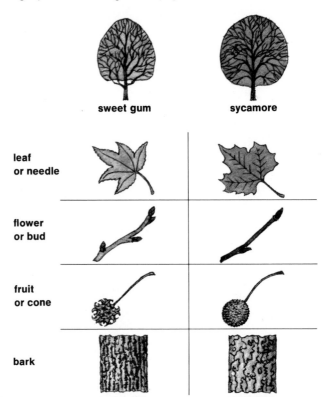

	sweet gum	sycamore
leaf or needle		
flower or bud		
fruit or cone		
bark		

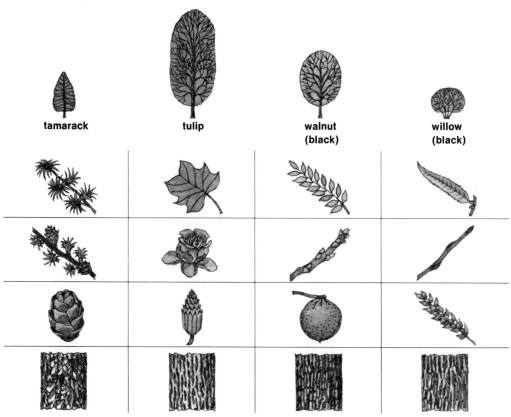

tamarack

tulip

**walnut
(black)**

**willow
(black)**

Did you take the wrong path? Look at these clues
to find your mistake. Start the game on page 180.

sweet gum

tulip

willow

tamarack

sycamore

walnut

Solving tree mysteries

How would you like to be a tree detective? To be a tree detective you have to be able to use clues to find out the names of the trees you see.

You can use the tree charts on pages 180–193 to help you in your detective work. These charts show more than 40 common trees. Under each tree's name and picture, the parts of that kind of tree are shown—its leaf or needle, its flower or bud, its fruit or cone, and its bark.

Take this book with you when you start your detective work. There are probably several kinds of trees growing near your house. Look first at a tree's leaves. They're your first clue. Compare a leaf with the leaves shown in the identification chart. If you can find a picture that looks like your leaf, you're getting warm.

Next, look at the bark on your tree. Does it look like the picture of the bark that's under the leaf picture? If it doesn't, you're barking up the wrong tree. Keep looking at the chart. Can you find on the chart a tree that has a leaf, bark, and other things that look just like those on the real tree? If you can, you've solved the mystery! You've learned the tree's name!

Leaf-scar faces

Some trees have "faces"! You can see them in the fall, if you look closely.

When leaves drop off a tree, scars are left. The scars often look like the faces of animals—or even creatures from another planet. They appear where new leaves will grow, so they are called leaf-scar faces.

Different trees have different leaf-scar faces. Four kinds are shown on these pages. What do you think they look like?

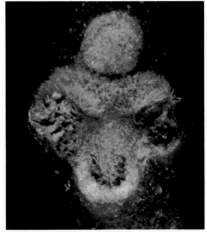

butternut leaf-scar face

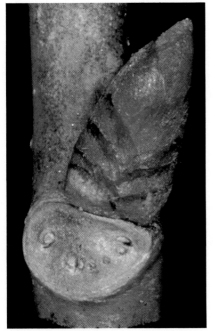

elm leaf-scar face

ash leaf-scar face

◀ **poplar leaf-scar face**

Christmas tree favorites

Which is your favorite kind of Christmas tree?

People in the United States and Canada usually choose the balsam fir, the black spruce, or the Douglas fir. People in Britain, Germany, and most of Europe like the silver fir and the Norway spruce. And the hardy Scots (or Scotch) pine is becoming a favorite with many people in both North America and Europe.

You can tell these trees by their shapes, by their needles, and by their cones.

balsam fir

silver fir

Douglas fir

Norway spruce

Scots (Scotch) pine

black spruce

Plants of Long Ago

Do you know that the very first living thing on land came out of the water?

Do you know that there was no soil in the world until the plants of long ago made some?

And, do you know that we couldn't live on the land today if the plants of long ago hadn't made the kind of air we breathe?

Many of the plants of long ago were strange looking. Many of them weren't very pretty. But we owe a lot to the plants of long ago. They helped to make the world we know today.

Long ago, the land was empty. All the plants and animals lived in the water. They looked like tiny blobs of jelly.

The first plants

Many hundreds of millions of years ago, the world was a scary place! Fiery volcanoes boomed and rumbled. The sky was filled with black ash. There was nothing but huge, gray ocean and miles and miles of bare, rocky land. There was no living thing *anywhere* on the land—not one plant or animal of any kind!

But in the seas there were millions of living creatures. They were so tiny you couldn't have seen them without a microscope. They looked like drops of jelly filled with bubbles.

Many of these tiny creatures were green. They were plants—the first plants in the world.

The air makers

Every sunny day the tiny green plants that lived in the ocean hundreds of millions of years ago were busy. They made their food with the help of sunlight, just as green plants still do.

As the tiny plants made their food, they gave off a gas called oxygen. Each tiny puff of oxygen made a bubble in the water. The bubbles rose to the top of the water and burst. The puffs of gas went into the air.

For millions of years, hundreds of billions of tiny plants made tiny puffs of oxygen. Finally, the air of the world was filled with oxygen.

The only reason we breathe air is to get the oxygen that's in it. Our bodies must have oxygen. Without it we would die. Without oxygen in the air, every plant and animal that lives on land would die.

If there had been no plants to put oxygen into the air millions of years ago, there probably would be no living things on the land today!

Ancient plants like these made the oxygen that made life on land possible.

The plants that conquered the land

The first living thing on land came out of the water.

Some 500 million years ago there wasn't a single living thing anywhere on land. But there were many kinds of living things in the sea. There were jellyfish, sponges, worms, and crablike animals called trilobites. And there were plants that grew in shallow water near the shore.

Slowly, as many years passed, the plants grew toward the shore. At last they were growing right out of the water, creeping onto the land. They didn't look like much—probably like bunches of flat leaves or stubby green stems. But they were the first things in the world to live on the land.

Plants that came out of the water were the first living things on land. These plants helped to make the first soil.

The soil makers

Hundreds of millions of years ago, all the land was just bare, hard rock, sand, or clay. Now, soil covers most of the land. Where did the soil come from?

Plants and weather made it. The first living things on land were plants that grew out of water onto wet rocks. The plants pushed tiny roots into cracks in the rocks. Slowly, with the help of wind and rain, the roots broke the rocks and crumbled them into tiny pieces.

As plants died, they too broke into tiny pieces. And this mixture of crumbled rock and dead plants lying on the wet rocks was the first soil.

The first plants to live on land helped make the first soil in which other plants could live and grow. And every plant that has lived and died since, has helped make more of the soil that now covers most of the land.

The snaky plants

About 400 million years ago, the plants on land looked like snakes with stalks on their backs.

The long, snaky, rootlike stems of these plants curled over the ground. Tiny hairs grew out of the stems and reached into the ground to find water. Scaly stalks without leaves or flowers grew up out of the stems. The stalks were about three feet high.

There were no trees or grass or flowers anywhere. Just the strange, snaky plants, growing on the shores of lakes and quiet pools of water.

Use this small picture to find out the names of the plants in the big picture.

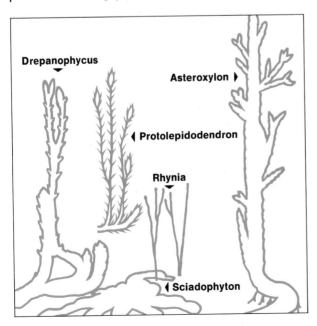

whisk fern

This plant looks very much like some of the plants that lived 400 million years ago.

Strange trees!

Have you ever seen a tree that looked like a giant asparagus stalk? Or one that had leaves on its trunk instead of bark?

That's what some of the trees looked like about 350 million years ago. They grew close together in swampy places and made the world's first forests.

None of those strange trees grew more than 40 feet tall. That's not very big for a tree. Oaks, elms, and other trees of today usually grow to be more than 80 feet tall.

Use this small picture to find out the names of the plants in the big picture.

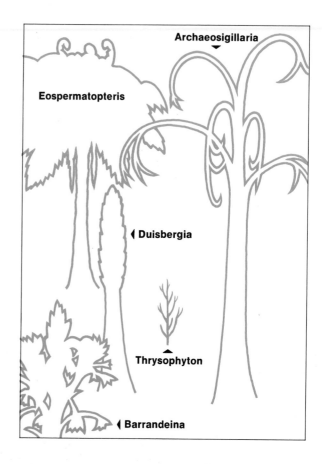

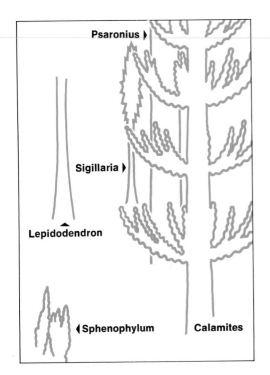

Psaronius ▶

Sigillaria ▶

Lepidodendron ▲

◀ Sphenophylum   Calamites

Use this small picture
to find out the names of the
plants in the big picture.

horsetails

Today, horsetails are small. But millions
of years ago, they were 50-foot giants.

The forests that turned to coal

The air was hot and wet. The ground was soft and oozy. Dragonflies with wings as long as your arm hummed through the air. Cockroaches as big as your fist hurried about. And, growing thickly everywhere, were strange towering trees and other plants.

That's what a forest was like during the Coal Age, 300 million years ago.

We call it the Coal Age because the trees and plants that grew then became the coal we use today. The plants in these forests grew and died and fell down. They were quickly covered by other plants that died and fell. All these dead plants were squeezed together. Slowly, during millions of years, they became the coal we burn for heat.

Some of the trees in the coal forests looked like Christmas trees. Others weren't like trees at all—they were strange, giant plants. One of them was an ancient relative of the little plant called a horsetail, that grows near lakes and ponds today. Today's horsetails grow only about 3 feet tall. But the horsetails that grew in the coal forests were giants, more than 50 feet tall.

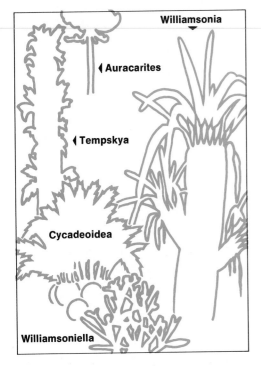

Williamsonia

◀ Auracarites

◀ Tempskya

Cycadeoidea

Williamsoniella

Use this small picture
to find out the names of the
plants in the big picture.

Plants the dinosaurs saw

You can see some kinds of plants that dinosaurs saw!

The giant dinosaurs of 150 million years ago lived in forests of conifers, cycads, and ginkgo trees. And all these kinds of plants are still living in the world.

Conifers are trees that have cones, such as pine and fir trees. A cycad looks somewhat like a fat pineapple with a circle of feathers sticking out of its top. Cycads were once common, but now they grow only in a few warm places in the world.

Ginkgoes are tall, pointed trees with lacy branches full of leaves like little fans. Ginkgo trees have been planted in many cities in America and other parts of the world. Look for a ginkgo tree in your town or city. You'll see the same kind of tree the dinosaurs saw.

ginkgo tree

Ginkgo trees look just as they
did 150 million years ago,
when dinosaurs were alive.

A changing world

By about 50 million years ago, many of the plants had become like the ones we have now. There was grass on the ground. And there were trees, bushes, and flowers like those you see today.

Animals had changed, too. The dinosaurs were all gone. The animals were more like the kinds of animals that live today.

The plants and animals of the world are always changing. They have changed many times and will change again. But these changes happen too slowly to be seen. It's a process that takes millions of years and that never stops happening.

Use this small picture to find out the names of the plants in the big picture.

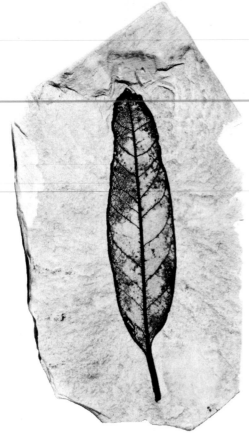

fossil of a 20-million-year-old plant

fossil of a 30-million-year-old plant

fossil of a 100-million-year-old plant

fossil of a 300-million-year-old plant

Looking at plants of long ago

How would you like to see a *real* leaf that might have been touched by a dinosaur—a leaf that's more than 100 million years old? It seems almost impossible, but such leaves really have been found!

Leaves of long-ago plants fell to the ground, just as leaves do today. Sometimes the leaves fell into streams and rivers. The water carried them along and finally buried them in mudbanks.

After many years the streams dried up. The mudbanks hardened into rock. And the leaves were pressed tight inside the rock. But by soaking the rock with acid, and splitting it, we can see the leaves—leaves that still have the same shape they had millions of years ago!

Sometimes leaves and other parts of long-ago plants left prints in the mud, just as you can make a print by pressing something into clay. When the mud hardened into rock, the prints were still there. And sometimes leaves, flowers, and even tree trunks were turned into coal or stone.

All these leaves, and prints, and parts of plants that have changed to stone and coal are called fossils. And it is from these fossils that we know what the plants of long ago were like.

fossil of a 300-million-year-old plant

What Plants Do for Us

Plants do a lot for us. We couldn't live without them.

Plants give us most of the foods we eat. Vegetables, fruits, cereals, flour, sugar, spices, and syrups all come from plants.

Plants give us wood for building houses and making furniture.

From plants we get cotton, linen, and other kinds of cloth for our clothing, handkerchiefs, bedspreads, and tablecloths.

Plants give us paper and rubber and string and medicines to make us well.

Plants even give us the fresh air we breathe!

And—just as important—plants give us pleasure. For, what sort of a world would it be if there were no shady trees, green grass, or lovely flowers?

Fresh air to breathe

Every green plant in the world is a kind of factory. It works away, all day long, making food for itself. As it does this, it gives off tiny streams of a gas called oxygen. This oxygen mixes with the other gases that make up the air.

Oxygen is very important! We, and all other animals, must have oxygen in order to live. Without oxygen, we would quickly die. We breathe air to get the oxygen that is in it.

All people and other animals that live on land take oxygen out of the air when they breathe. You might think that all the oxygen would soon be used up, and so it would be, if it weren't for the green plants! They keep putting fresh oxygen into the air.

So, without the green plant factories to give us a fresh supply of oxygen, we couldn't live!

oxygen experiment

This experiment shows an elodea plant making oxygen. The plant is in a jar filled with water. A glass funnel is over the plant, and a test tube is over the funnel. You can see a bubble in the water in the test tube. It's a bubble of oxygen just made by the plant. Because oxygen is a gas, it rises up through the water.

More and more bubbles of oxygen go up through the water to the top of the test tube. The oxygen slowly pushes the water out of the test tube and into the jar. Soon, the top of the test tube is filled with oxygen that came from the elodea plant.

Seeds, stems, and salad stuff

All the foods we call vegetables come from some part of a plant.

Lima beans, peas, and kidney beans are plant seeds.

Radishes, carrots, and beets are plant roots.

Onions are plant bulbs. Potatoes are the underground stems of a plant.

Celery and rhubarb are the stalks of plants.

Broccoli and cauliflower are the flowers, buds, and stems of plants. Cabbage is the bud of a plant.

Lettuce is the leaves of a plant.

And string beans and scarlet runners are the whole fruits of plants, even though we call them vegetables.

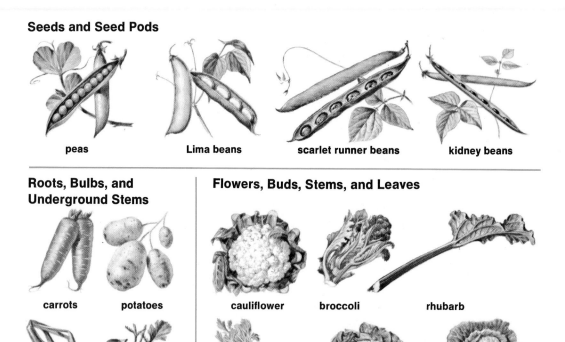

Seeds and Seed Pods

peas Lima beans scarlet runner beans kidney beans

Roots, Bulbs, and Underground Stems

carrots potatoes

onion radishes

Flowers, Buds, Stems, and Leaves

cauliflower broccoli rhubarb

celery lettuce cabbage

Sweet and tasty seed packages

Anything that grows on a plant and has seeds inside it is a fruit. A fruit is really just a package with one or more plant seeds in it.

Many kinds of fruits are good to eat. Apples, oranges, pears, peaches, plums, and dates are sweet seed packages that come from trees. Blueberries, gooseberries, strawberries, raspberries, and huckleberries are the seed packages of shrubs. Grapes, cranberries, and watermelons are the seed packages of vines.

Cucumbers, squash, pumpkins, and tomatoes are tasty packages of seeds, too. Even though we call them vegetables, they are really fruits!

Fruits

apple   orange   peach   date

blackberry   grapes   watermelon

Fruits We Call Vegetables

cucumber   pumpkin   tomato

Bread, breakfast food, and popcorn

Do you know that you probably eat grass?

When we think of grass we usually think of green lawns. But there are many kinds of grass. Wheat, oats, rye, barley, rice, and corn (which is called maize in many parts of the world) are all grasses. These grasses are called cereals. And their fruits, which we eat, are called grains.

Grains are one of the most important foods we get from plants. Without grains we wouldn't have bread, cookies, breakfast cereals, rice for chop suey—or popcorn to munch on at the movies!

Sugar, syrup, and spices

Most sugar comes from different parts of two plants. Some sugar comes from the long, white root of the sugar-beet plant. Some sugar comes from the juicy stem of the sugar-cane plant, which is a kind of grass.

All syrup and honey come from plants. Maple syrup is the sap of the sugar maple tree. Molasses is made from sugar-cane juice. Honey is made by bees from the nectar of many kinds of flowers.

Nearly all the spices that make your tongue tingle come from plants, too. Pepper is the dried, ground-up berries of a shrub. Cinnamon is the bark of a tree. Mustard, which goes so well on a hot dog, is made from the ground-up seeds of a small plant with yellow flowers. And most other spices are the dried leaves, stems, flowers, or seeds of little plants called herbs.

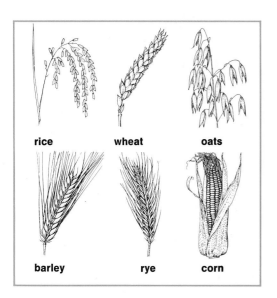

rice   wheat   oats

barley   rye   corn

Bread, breakfast food, and popcorn are all made from the fruit of plants called cereals.

harvesting wheat

Sugar, syrup, and honey all come from plants. So do pepper, mustard, and most other spices.

cutting sugar cane

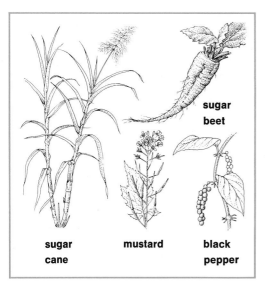

sugar beet

sugar cane   mustard   black pepper

licorice

The flavor of licorice candy comes from this plant's roots.

peppermint

Peppermint candy gets its flavor from this plant.

spearmint

Candy and gum are flavored by oil from this plant.

wintergreen

Wintergreen flavor comes from this plant.

Party treats from plants

Some of our favorite party treats get their flavors from plants.

Do you like licorice candy? Licorice is a flavor made from the root of the licorice plant. Peppermint, spearmint, and wintergreen are flavors made from oils that come from little plants. And vanilla flavor comes from the fruit of an orchid!

We can thank trees for some of our best treats. The nuts that go into fudge, fruit cake, pies, cakes, cookies, and ice cream are all tree seeds! So, of course, are the crunchy cashews and other nuts we eat salted or plain.

Some tree seeds give us a treat in a different way. We don't eat kola nuts, but from them we get the flavor for fizzy cola drinks. And from cacao beans, which are really tree seeds, too, we get chocolate.

The nut you probably like best—the peanut—isn't a nut at all. In fact, it isn't even a tree seed. It's a kind of pea.

All of these nuts, except the peanut, are the seeds of trees. The peanut is really a pea, and comes from a little leafy plant. ▶

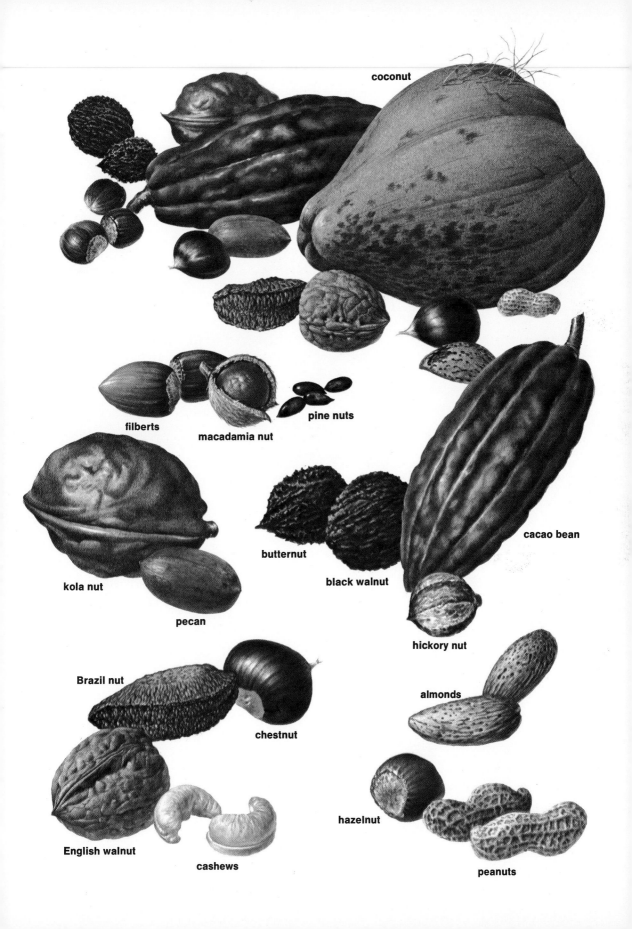

coconut

filberts

macadamia nut

pine nuts

kola nut

pecan

butternut

black walnut

cacao bean

hickory nut

Brazil nut

chestnut

almonds

English walnut

cashews

hazelnut

peanuts

sawmill

At sawmills, big tree trunks are cut up into boards. These are used for houses, furniture, and other products.

Baseball bats and hockey sticks

Houses, tables, chairs, and floors,
Rowboats, pencils, desks, and doors,
Baseball bats and hockey sticks,
Boxes for magicians' tricks.
Each and every one of these
Is made of wood that comes from trees!

Dresses, shirts, and tablecloths

Do you have a cotton dress or a cotton shirt? Cotton comes from the seeds of the cotton plant. The seeds are covered with fine fuzz that we twist into thread and weave into cloth.

Does your mother have a fine linen tablecloth? Linen is made from the stalks of the flax plant.

cotton plant

When cotton fruit is ripe, it pops open. Then the seeds, covered with white fuzz, are harvested.

harvesting cotton

Stalks of flax plants are dried, scraped, and combed into long strips to be spun into thread.

drying flax stalks

flax plant

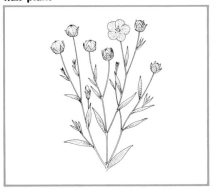

Medicines to make you well

If you get sick, a plant may help you get well. Many medicines that doctors give sick people are made from plants.

One of the best medicines is penicillin. It cures so many kinds of sickness that it's called a wonder drug. Penicillin comes from plants called molds that grow on bread and fruit.

Different kinds of plants are used to make cough syrups, tonics, and many other medicines that the doctor may give you to take when you don't feel well.

There is one very strange thing about the plants that medicines come from. Most of these plants are poisonous! If you ate one of them you would probably become very sick. You might even die. But when these plants are used in medicines, they help you get well!

foxglove

People with heart trouble use a medicine made from this plant.

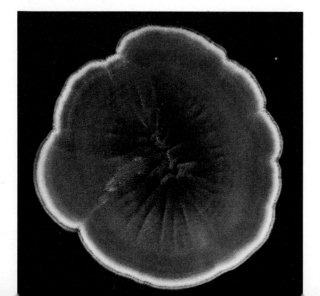

penicillium mold

The medicine called penicillin is made from a mold such as this.

Books, tires, and string

The next time you read a book, ride a bicycle, or fly a kite, thank the plants! Without them, you might not be able to do any of those things.

The paper in most books comes from trees. To make paper, wood chips from trees are cooked into a soupy pulp. Then this mixture is squeezed into sheets and dried. Rags of linen or cotton, which also come from plants, are used to make very fine paper.

Bicycle tires and many other things are made from natural or man-made rubber. Natural rubber comes from the milky, white juice of the rubber tree. When the juice is taken from the tree it becomes hard and bouncy. Artificial rubber is made from chemicals, but some of the chemicals come from plants, too.

Kite string is usually made from cotton, which comes from the long threads on seeds of the cotton plant. But most string and rope is made from the veins, called fibers, of long plant leaves. These fibers are removed from the leaves and dried. Then they are twisted together to make rope, string, cord, or twine.

rubber tree

Rubber comes from the juice that flows when a rubber tree is cut.

These swordlike sisal leaves will be used to make string and rope.

sisal plants

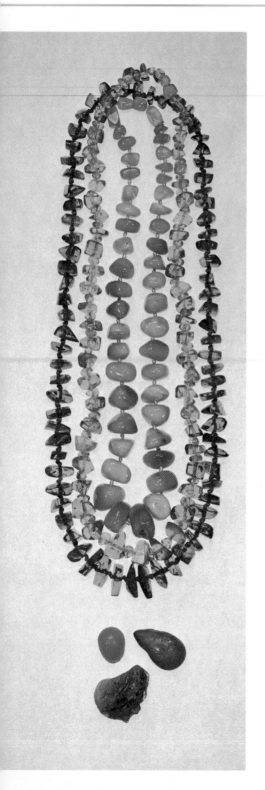

Jewels, color, perfume, and music

From plants we get jewelry, perfumes, colors, and even music!

Necklaces and other jewelry are often made of a yellowish rock called amber. And amber came from a plant. Once, it was a sticky gum from trees like our pine and spruce trees. This gum turned hard as rock, millions of years ago.

The perfume your mother sometimes puts on probably came from a plant, too. The best kinds of perfumes are made of oil that comes from flowers.

Not long ago, people used the juice of flowers, berries, and bark to give different colors to cloth. Some of these things are still used, but most colors are now made from coal tar. These coal tar dyes come from plants, too, because coal comes from trees that died long, long ago.

We get music from plants, too. The violins and clarinets in big orchestras, and the guitars of folk and rock musicians are made of wood that comes from trees.

amber necklaces

Amber is the hardened juice of trees that died millions of years ago. When it is polished, it makes beautiful jewelry. Below these amber necklaces are three chunks of unpolished amber.

Colors We Get from Plants

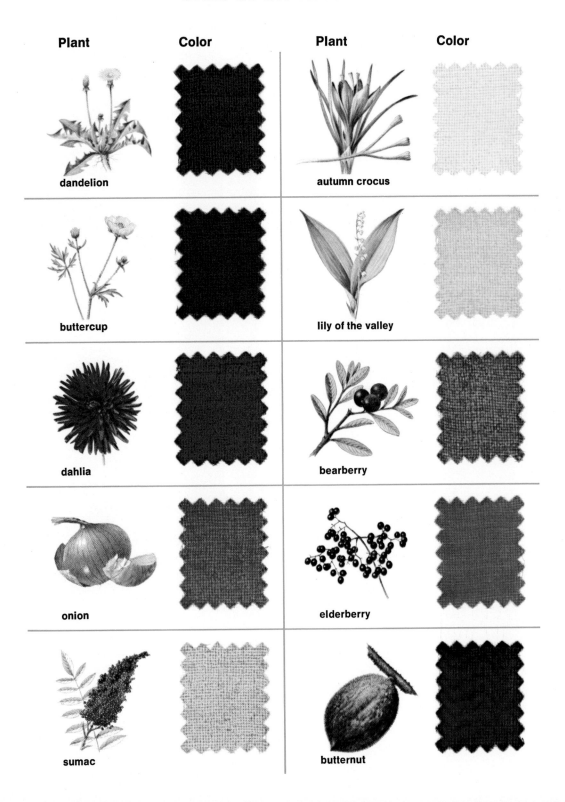

Plant	Color	Plant	Color
dandelion		autumn crocus	
buttercup		lily of the valley	
dahlia		bearberry	
onion		elderberry	
sumac		butternut	

A bright and beautiful world

It's nice to have shady trees around you on a hot, summer day.

It's nice to see the bright faces of flowers nodding at you, and to smell their sweet scent.

It's nice to have cool grass to walk on with bare feet.

Green things make the world seem brighter. We need them around us. Their beauty gives us pleasure and adds to our happiness.

People and Plants

There are a great many kinds of jobs for people who like to work with plants.

Botanists, biologists, biochemists, and agronomists are scientists who study plants. They look for ways to grow better, healthier food plants, or ways to make new, useful things from plants, or ways to use plants to help cure diseases.

Horticulturists, foresters, gardeners, and landscapers are people who plant and care for the flowers and trees you see in parks, gardens, and along city streets.

Florists make it possible for us to have beautiful flowers for special occasions. Seed growers make it possible for us to plant gardens.

There are also many artists and photographers who spend much of their time painting or taking pictures of plants for calendars, magazines, and books.

People who study plants

Do you ever wonder about plants, and how they live and grow? Have you ever taken a flower apart to see what was inside it? If you have wondered about, or done these things, maybe someday you'll be a botanist!

Botanists are scientists who try to find out all about plants. The work of botanists has given us more and better food plants. And it has helped other scientists to make medicine and other useful things from plants.

botanist in a laboratory

Botanists are scientists who study plants. Sometimes they work outside, but they often do experiments in laboratories.

botanist in Africa

Botanists often go to far-off places to find new kinds of plants that may be useful.

Some botanists study underwater plants. They work with other scientists to see if any of these plants might be used for food.

botanist under water

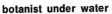

People who find new ways to use plants

Of course, you know that fruits, vegetables, rubber, string, and several kinds of cloth come from plants. But do you know that the clear, smooth cellophane that mother sometimes wraps things in comes from plants, too? And so does the margarine you spread on bread.

Scientists called chemists made these things. In laboratories all over the world, chemists are working to find new, useful things that can be made from plants.

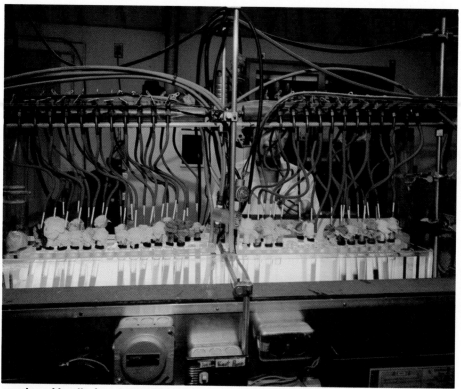

growing chlorella in a laboratory

In this laboratory, chemists are working to make a new kind of food from a water plant called chlorella.

Dr. George Washington Carver

Dr. George Washington Carver was a great
scientist who found many new ways to use
plants. He made more than 100 different
things from corn. And from peanuts he
made more than 300 different things, such
as paper, face cream, flour—and even milk!

People who work with farm plants

If you had a sick pet, you would take it to an animal doctor called a veterinarian. And if you were a farmer with sick plants or poor soil, you would get help from a plant doctor called an agronomist.

Agronomists are scientists who find ways of making soil grow more things, and of making plants larger and healthier. The work they do helps farmers raise more food to feed people around the world.

agronomist in the field

An American agronomist shows farmers in Ghana how to make their crops healthier.

agronomist in a laboratory

This agronomist is testing many different kinds of soil to see which is best for these plants.

People who work in forests

Wouldn't it be fun to live in the woods? That's what many foresters and forest rangers get to do!

There are two kinds of foresters and forest rangers. One kind works for a government. It's their job to take care of the national parks and forests so that there will always be places where people can go camping, sightseeing, hunting, and fishing.

Other foresters work in woods that are owned by lumber companies. Their job is to see that there are plenty of trees from which tables, chairs, doors, baseball bats, and other wooden things can be made.

Both kinds of foresters do the same kind of work. They protect the trees from insects, animals, and diseases that might damage them. They cut down old trees and plant new ones. They help trees make new seeds.

One of a forester's most important jobs is to guard against fire, for a fire can destroy a whole forest. Often, a forester will spend days on a lookout station, high on a mountainside. Here he watches for smoke that will warn of a fire starting. Then the forester directs the firefighters in their struggle against the forest's terrible enemy!

forester at work

This forester is putting pollen on the cones of a Douglas fir tree to make new seeds grow.

People who help gardens to grow

Lots of people like to garden for fun. But there are people who work as gardeners and get paid! They work in parks, zoos, and many other public places where there are trees and other plants to care for.

Gardeners and landscapers also work for towns and cities. They are the men who plant and care for the trees, bushes, and beds of flowers that you see along streets and around many public buildings.

landscapers at work

Landscapers often use special tools to dig up trees and replant them in other places.

gardeners at work

These Dutch gardeners are growing tulips for bulbs. The bulbs will be sold to other gardeners all over the world.

People who help us enjoy plants

A florist is an artist and gardener combined. Florists grow and sell plants and flowers. They also make the beautiful bouquets you see at weddings, anniversaries, and on other special occasions.

florist in a greenhouse

Florist shops are beautiful,
All damply green and dimly cool,
And the men who keep them are sure to be
A little baggy about the knee,
With voices pleasant and rather low
From living along with things that grow;
For you can't stay noisy and hurried where
Petal on petal fills the air
With spiciness, and every tree
Is hung with gayest greenery.
Grocers bustle and butchers shout,
Tradesmen tramp noisily in and out,
But florists are quiet men and kind,
With a sort of fragrance of the mind.

florist arranging flowers ▶

THE FLORIST SHOP
Rachel Field

People who make pictures of plants

Pictures of plants are often needed for magazines, calendars, and books like this one. Many of these pictures are taken by photographers who specialize in photographing plants.

Sometimes, plant pictures are needed that can't be taken by a photographer. Those pictures are made by artists who have made a special study of plants. They can paint pictures that look as real as photographs.

artist Alex Ebel

Alex Ebel specializes in painting pictures of plants and animals that lived millions of years ago. All of the exciting pictures in the section of this book called "Plants of Long Ago" were painted by Mr. Ebel.

photographer David Muench

David Muench enjoys taking pictures that
show the beautiful shapes and designs that
are often found in plants. You can see
some of Mr. Muench's plant photographs on
pages 110, 111, 114, 282, and 288.

True Tales and Tall Tales

Have you ever read a story in which the hero was a plant?

The people of Scotland tell such a story. It's about how a plant called a thistle saved a Scottish king.

Have you ever heard about the plant that people hunt for with pigs? Or about the girl who turned into a plant? Or about the country that was nearly ruined by a plant?

There are lots of stories about plants. Some of them are true and some are make-believe. A few of them have been retold for you, here.

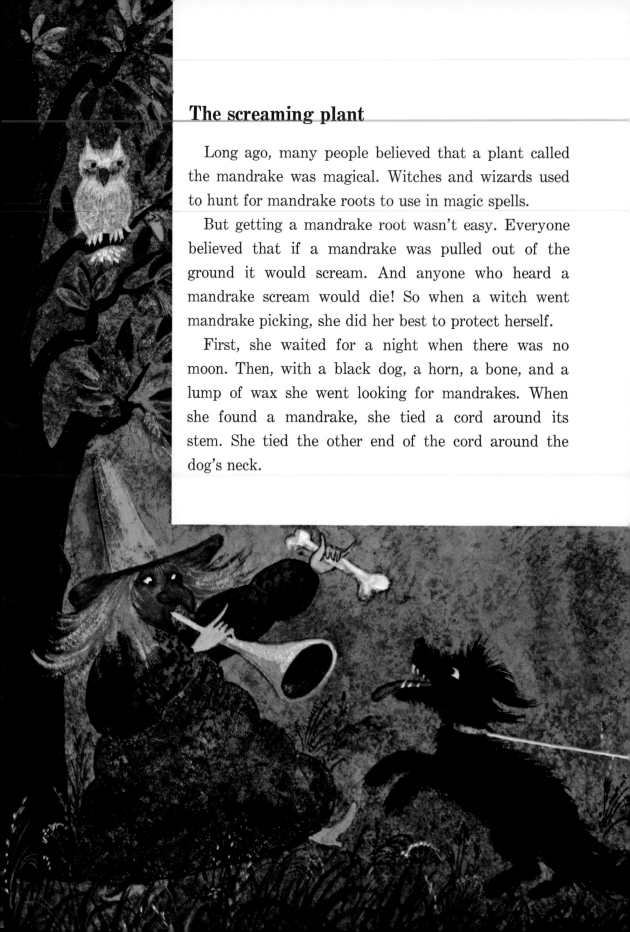

The screaming plant

Long ago, many people believed that a plant called the mandrake was magical. Witches and wizards used to hunt for mandrake roots to use in magic spells.

But getting a mandrake root wasn't easy. Everyone believed that if a mandrake was pulled out of the ground it would scream. And anyone who heard a mandrake scream would die! So when a witch went mandrake picking, she did her best to protect herself.

First, she waited for a night when there was no moon. Then, with a black dog, a horn, a bone, and a lump of wax she went looking for mandrakes. When she found a mandrake, she tied a cord around its stem. She tied the other end of the cord around the dog's neck.

Then the witch stuffed her ears with some of the wax and waited. At exactly midnight she held out the bone to the dog. The dog ran to get the bone—and pulled the mandrake out of the ground. But the witch was safe. She couldn't hear the mandrake scream because her ears were stuffed up and she was blowing the horn as loudly as she could.

Today, of course, we know how silly all that was. There's no such thing as a magical plant, because there's no such thing as magic. The witch or wizard wouldn't have heard the mandrake scream anyway, because mandrakes, or any other plants, can't make noise. And now we know that there are no wizards and witches—and that there never have been.

mandrake

Long ago, people thought that this plant would scream like a person if it was pulled out of the ground.

The plant that saved a king

Thistles aren't the sort of flower that people like to pick. They aren't very pretty and they have prickly leaves that hurt you if you touch them. And thistles grow so quickly and thickly that they are pests to farmers.

But the ugly, prickly thistle is an honored plant in Scotland. This is because there is an old Scottish legend that tells how thistles once saved a Scottish king from the Vikings.

Vikings were fierce warriors who came from the northern countries of Sweden, Denmark, and Norway. The Vikings loved war and fighting. They sailed to different parts of the world and attacked towns and castles. They often killed all the people, stole all the riches, and burned everything down.

An old story tells how some Vikings landed in Scotland more than a thousand years ago. During the night they surrounded the Scottish king's castle. Everyone in the castle was asleep. They didn't know the Vikings were about to attack.

All around the castle there was a moat—a deep, wide pit. Moats were usually filled with water, so the Vikings took off their sandals to wade across the moat. But this moat wasn't filled with water. It was dry, and it was filled with thousands of prickly thistles!

When the first barefoot Vikings stepped on those thistles they howled with pain! The noise woke the people in the castle, who were able to defeat the Vikings and chase them away. Today, the thistle is the national emblem of Scotland.

Scottish thistle

The thistle is the national flower of Scotland.

The flower that tells of battles

More than a thousand years ago, says an old French tale, there lived a holy man now known as Saint Leonard. One day he gave away all his money and everything he owned. Then he went to live by himself in a valley in a forest.

But a dragon named Temptation also lived in that valley. This dragon was a huge creature that breathed fire, looked like a snake, and had wings like a bat. The dragon Temptation attacked Saint Leonard, but the holy man chased it away. Saint Leonard and the dragon fought many terrible battles, and the dragon always lost. The holy man chased the beast farther and farther toward the edge of the woods. And, finally, the dragon disappeared forever from the valley.

But a strange thing happened where each of the battles was fought. Wherever drops of Saint Leonard's blood fell to the ground, flowers grew! These flowers were called lilies of the valley, in honor of Saint Leonard's battles in the valley against the dragon Temptation.

lily of the valley

In a French legend, these flowers first grew where drops of a saint's blood fell.

The hunting of the truffle

Truffles are plants that grow underground. That makes them hard to find. But truffles are so tasty that people often spend long hours hunting for them. Some people even train animals to help them hunt for truffles. And some of the best truffle hunters are pigs.

Let's pretend you're going on a truffle hunt. First, you must go out into the woods where truffles grow. It's a long walk, and if your pig had to walk all the way, it might be too tired to hunt. So you have to carry the pig in your arms! Or, maybe you pull it in a wagon!

When you get to where you think the truffles are, you tie a rope around the pig's neck. Then you hold on to

the other end of the rope and follow the pig as he starts to hunt. He sniffles and snuffles in search of the truffles. When he smells one, he begins to dig.

Now pigs like truffles as much as people do. To keep your pig from eating the truffles, you must quickly drag him away. But you have to give him a reward for finding the truffles, or he may stop hunting. So you give him an acorn. Then you tie him to a tree and dig up the truffles. They won't look like much—just little, wrinkled, brown balls with warts on them! But in England, France, and other countries in Europe where truffles grow, people pay lots of money for them!

truffles

Truffles grow underground.
They are good to eat,
so people hunt for them.

The girl who became a flower

Long ago, the people in Greece believed that the sun was a god named Helios, who drove across the sky in a chariot pulled by four horses. There is a Greek tale about a girl named Clytie who fell in love with Helios. She loved him so much that all she wanted to do was watch as Helios drove across the sky.

All day long, Clytie sat on the ground, watching the sun. She never looked at anything else. She never moved. Even when night came, she stayed where she was, just waiting for the sun to rise.

For nine days and nine nights Clytie did not eat any food. She drank only her tears and the dew from the leaves of near-by plants. And on the tenth day her body took root in the ground. It became a flower stem. Her face became a flower that turned slowly on its stem, still watching the sun move across the sky.

The flower is named the heliotrope. In Greek, this means "turning toward the sun." And true to its name, the beautiful, sweet-scented heliotrope blossom always turns toward the sun.

heliotrope

In Greek legend, this flower was once a girl.

The flower that nearly ruined a country

Imagine paying thousands of dollars for a flower that hadn't even grown yet! That's what many people did about 300 years ago in Holland. Tulips were new to Holland then, and rich people were willing to pay lots of money to have tulips in their gardens. Tulips grow from underground buds called bulbs, and many Dutchmen saw that they could make money by selling tulip bulbs.

But it takes three to seven years to raise tulip bulbs from seeds. Some people didn't want to wait that long. They wanted money right away. So they began to sell bulbs *before* they had them! A tulip bulb grower would sell some bulbs he didn't yet have to a man for a thousand dollars in Dutch money. That man would sell the bulbs he didn't yet have to someone else for twice as much. And that person would sell the bulbs *he* didn't yet have for three times as much!

Tulip bulb prices went higher and higher. Some people even sold their houses to get money to buy tulip bulbs to sell. People traded valuable things for tulip bulbs. One tulip bulb was sold for 4 cows, 8 pigs, 12 sheep, 2 barrels of butter, 1,000 pounds of cheese, 2 big barrels of wine, 4 barrels of beer, 2 wagonloads of wheat, a bed, a suit of clothes, and a large silver cup!

Suddenly, people became afraid to spend so much on tulip bulbs. Prices dropped. People who had bought tulip bulbs couldn't sell them. Many of these people lost all their money. Others lost their houses. The country of Holland was nearly ruined—by tulips!

tulip bulbs

A bulb is an underground bud. The leaves and stem of a tulip grow right out of the bulb.

Saving the Plants

Conservation is a word that means "saving things that come from nature"—air, soil, water, animals, *and* plants.

It might seem as if plants don't need care, but they do. Plants can get sick, just as people can. Insects can chew up a plant's leaves or roots until it dies. Fire can turn a forest into a pile of ashes.

People and the things they make cause dangers, too. Polluted air from cars, trucks, and factories can choke the life out of plants. And plants lose space in which to live when ground is dug up for mines, factories, roads, and parking lots.

We need to save the plants. They give us beauty. They give us food. And they give us fresh air. We couldn't live without them!

That's why conservation is important.

smut on corn

Smut is a tiny plant called a fungus.
Many of these plants sometimes grow
on corn and make it rot and die.

Deadly enemies

Deadly enemies of plants lurk in the Green Kingdom!

They are tiny plants called fungi, that look somewhat like cobwebs. Not all fungi are deadly, but some are plant killers! They fasten themselves to plants and use them as food. The fungi grow and multiply, causing the other plants to become slimy and rotten. These plant-killing fungi have nasty-sounding names such as smut, blight, rust, and mildew.

Can these little monsters cause trouble for people? They certainly can! In Ireland, about 125 years ago, a fungus called blight attacked the potato crop. And nearly a million Irish people starved to death because potatoes were their chief food!

Once, beautiful chestnut trees grew everywhere in North America. They're almost all gone now—killed by blight!

Most plants are helpless when fungi attack them. But men can help plants fight these little monsters. Scientists have found chemicals that help keep plants from being attacked. They have also learned how to raise plants that fungi will not attack. Scientists still work to find new and better ways to save plants from their deadly fungi enemies.

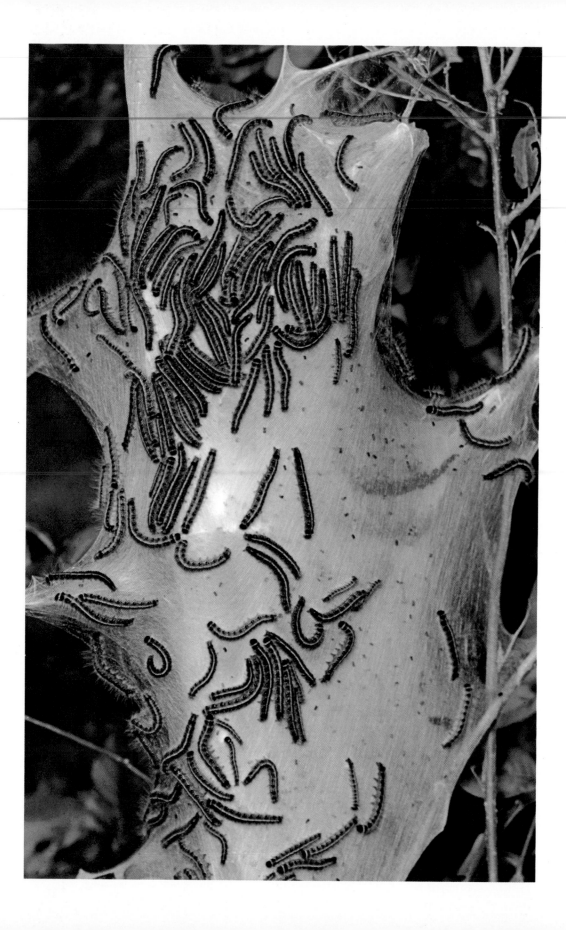

Insect enemies

Suppose you could make yourself as tiny as an insect. Then, suppose you sat on a leaf in a garden and were very still. You would probably hear a munching, crunching noise all around you. For, all summer long, day and night, billions of insects chew away at plants.

Many insects are truly plant enemies. And they're our enemies, too, for their food is often the same as ours—corn, wheat, tomatoes, potatoes, and fruit.

There are several ways to protect plants from insects. Some people use poison sprays, but many of these sprays are dangerous. Gardeners and farmers know that one of the best ways to protect plants from insects is with other insects!

Once, little insects called aphids were damaging alfalfa crops in California. The farmers turned thousands of ladybugs loose in their fields. The ladybugs gobbled up the aphids and saved the crops!

Using insects to fight insects is the safest way to protect plants. Scientists are looking for other ways. Getting rid of harmful insect enemies is important. But it has to be done with care. All insects, even those that attack plants, help to maintain the balance of nature.

tent caterpillars

Tent caterpillars are the deadly enemies of plants. A nest of tent caterpillars will often eat all the buds or young leaves on a tree. When this happens, the tree will die.

The enemy in the air

Imagine a world that is plain, even ugly —a world without beauty. Imagine a world in which most of the trees are dead. Many other plants are small and twisted. Leaves and flowers are spotted with disease. And fruits, such as grapes, apples, peaches, and plums, can't grow.

It wouldn't be a very nice world. But many scientists fear that's what our world is going to be like some day—if we don't do something about air pollution!

Air pollution can make you cough. It also makes your eyes water and sting. But it does far worse things to plants. It kills trees. It keeps flowers from budding. It spoils fruits and vegetables.

Air pollution is a very serious problem. But scientists and many other people are working on it. They're trying to clean up the air and keep it clean, for the sake of people *and* plants.

damaged aspen leaves

These leaves were damaged
by fumes from cars and trucks.

dead trees along a highway

Air pollution, caused by cars
and trucks, killed these trees
before they even began to grow.

mine or national park?

From open-pit mines such as the one in the top picture, we get a useful and important metal—copper. But this kind of mine destroys both land and plants. The bottom picture shows a place where valuable metals have been found. Some people want to dig an open-pit mine here. Others, who want to see the land stay the way it is, are trying to have the area declared a national park.

The most dangerous enemy

Plants and animals have one enemy more dangerous than any other. It isn't disease, or fire, or even pollution. The most dangerous enemy is—man!

Man is the only living creature that has ever caused another living creature to become extinct. The dodo, the great auk, and the passenger pigeon—hunted and killed by man—are gone from the world forever. Because of man, many other animals are nearly extinct. If they are not protected, they, too, will soon be gone—forever.

The same kind of thing is happening in the Green Kingdom. Plants need land upon which to grow. But people need roads, houses, factories, mines, shopping centers, and parking lots. So trees are chopped down, and land is cleared and paved. Little by little, the great forests, the coastal marshlands, and the wide, rolling prairies are disappearing.

We need the things that can be built on the land or taken out of it. But if we change too much land, we may upset the balance of nature. If this happens, man himself might become extinct. Men also need the natural beauty of unspoiled land. Without this beauty, men might lose their very love of life.

What to do? How do we solve this problem? How do we get what we need from the land and yet keep it the way it is? In one way, the answer seems simple. Save some land and use other land. But which land do we save and which do we use? People in government, industry, and private groups are trying to find an answer to this difficult question.

Fire!

The forest rangers are worried. The weather is hot and there has been no rain for a long time. They know the forest is as dry as sawdust. It would take only a tiny spark to turn the whole forest into a roaring, raging sea of fire!

Then, from their watchtower high above the trees, the rangers see a thin spiral of smoke. Fire! There's a fire in the forest!

A quick call for help goes out. Fire fighters rush to the blaze in trucks. Working as fast as they can, the men battle the blaze with streams of water and shovelfuls of dirt. They chop down trees and dig up the ground to keep the fire from spreading.

Overhead, airplanes swoop over the fire, dropping water and chemicals on it. From other planes come men with parachutes—fire fighters called smoke jumpers. They parachute into places that men on the ground can't reach easily. Dangerous work!

At last, after hours, or perhaps even days, the fire is out. Miles of forest, that might have become only ash-covered earth and blackened stumps, have been saved.

A forest is long in growing, but its ashes are made in a moment.

SENECA

planting a tree

Some children in Sacramento, California, got permission to make a park out of an empty lot. Working together, they planted more than a hundred trees and shrubs. The park will be kept wild and used as an outdoor classroom for nature study.

collecting wastepaper

Wastepaper can help save trees! It can be sold to mills that will make new paper from it. Then fewer trees will have to be cut down to be made into paper.

What you can do to help

You may think there's not much you can do to help save plants. But there are lots of things you can do! Here are just a few.

Save your family's old newspapers and wastepaper. Boy Scouts, Girl Scouts, and other groups often collect old paper. It can be sent to places that will make new paper from it. This means that fewer trees will be cut down to be made into paper.

If you have a lawn, help your father rake the leaves that fall on it in autumn. Don't burn them—that pollutes the air! Instead, rake them into a pile that's flat on top and leave them where rain can soak into them. They will rot and turn into dark, muddy-looking humus. Spread the humus on your lawn and it will make the soil richer for the grass and other plants.

Sometimes you can help plants by not doing things.

Don't peel bark from trees. The outside bark protects a tree from insects and fungus enemies. The inner bark moves food from the leaves to the roots. Peeling off a tree's bark may cause the tree to die.

When you pick wild flowers, don't take them all. Let some grow so that they can make seeds. Then, next year, there will be many more wild flowers for everyone to enjoy.

Look for a Lovely Thing

Look around you! The beauty of the Green Kingdom fills the world!

Meadows in spring are gay carpets of green and gold and pink. Autumn woodlands glow with fiery reds and purples. And in winter, the snow-covered branches of trees give forests a roof of silvery lace.

There's beauty in a bright, summer flower, splashed with sparkling raindrops. There's beauty in a dead, dry leaf, glinting with a touch of frost. There's beauty in bark and branches, in petals, stems, and seeds.

Beauty is all around you. The Green Kingdom makes the world a lovely place to live in.

cattails in moonlight

Look for a lovely thing and you will find it,
It is not far—
It never will be far.

from NIGHT
Sara Teasdale

desert cacti at daybreak

The mists of daybreak seem
To paint as with a fairy brush
A landscape in a dream.

Mists of Daybreak
Yosa Buson

pickerelweed in a pond

Rushes in a watery place,
And reeds in a hollow . . .

from RUSHES IN A WATERY PLACE
Christina Rossetti

quaking aspen leaf in midsummer

*When the wilderness is waking in a mist
of magian green . . .*

from GREEN FIRE
Bliss Carman

quaking aspen leaves in midwinter

The melancholy days are come,
the saddest of the year,
Of wailing winds and naked woods,
and meadows brown and sere.

from THE DEATH OF THE FLOWERS
William Cullen Bryant

fungi

iris

O Lord, how manifold are thy works!
In wisdom hast thou made them all:
The earth is full of thy riches.

PSALMS 104:24

squirreltail grass

To every thing there is a season,
And a time to every purpose under heaven:
A time to be born and a time to die . . .

ECCLESIASTES 3:1–2

black oak leaves

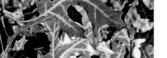

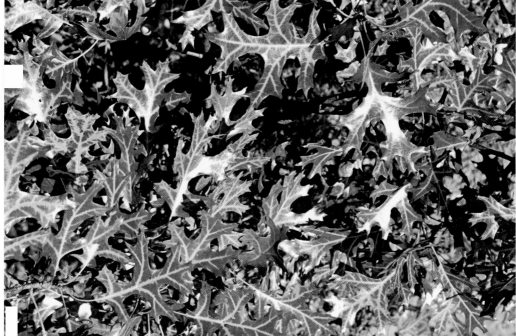

bristlecone pine bole

We paused amid the pines that stood
  The giants of the waste,
Tortured by storms to shapes as rude
  As serpents interlaced . . .

from THE RECOLLECTION
Percy Bysshe Shelley

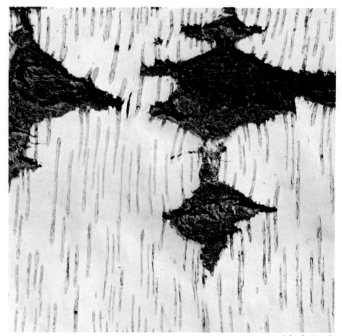

birch bark

"Lay aside your cloak, O Birch-tree!
Lay aside your white-skin wrapper,
For the Summer-time is coming,
and the sun is warm in heaven,
And you need no white-skin wrapper!"

from THE SONG OF HIAWATHA
Henry Wadsworth Longfellow

A thing of beauty is a joy for ever:
Its loveliness increases; it will never
Pass into nothingness . . .

From ENDYMION
John Keats

salsify

New Words

Here are some of the words you've met in this book. They may be new to you. Many of them are words you'll meet again in other books—so they're good words to know. Some of them are flower names that may be hard for you to pronounce. Next to each word you are shown how to say it correctly: acid (AS ihd). Put the emphasis on the part of the word shown in capital letters. Under each word, the meaning is given in a complete sentence.

acid (AS ihd)
An acid is a chemical substance strong enough to dissolve things.

agronomist (uh GRAHN uh mihst)
An agronomist is a person who studies how to improve the soil so that crops can grow better.

algae (AL jee)
Algae are green plants without stems, roots, or leaves. They live in water or moist soil and make their own food.

alyssum (uh LIHS uhm)
Alyssum is a plant of the mustard family. It has small yellow, pink, rose, or white flowers.

annual (AN you uhl)
An annual is a plant that lives only one year.

anther (AN thuhr)
The anther is a tiny sack on a stem inside a flower. The anthers hold the pollen.

biochemist (BY oh KEHM ihst)
A biochemist is a person who studies the actions and changes of substances in living things.

biologist (by AHL uh gihst)
A biologist is a person who studies living things.

biome (BY ohm)
In nature, a place where certain kinds of plants and animals live together is called a biome. The weather limits the kinds of plants and animals that can live there.

botanist (BAHT uh nihst)
A botanist is a person who studies plants.

broccoli (BRAHK uh lee)
Broccoli is an annual plant that is eaten as a vegetable.

bulrush (BULL ruhsh)
Bulrush is a tall, slender plant that grows in or near water.

cacao (kuh KAY oh)
The cacao is a kind of evergreen tree. Cocoa and chocolate are made from its seeds.

calamus (KAL uh muhs)
Calamus is a plant with long, sword-shaped leaves.

carbon dioxide (KAHR buhn dy AHK syde)
Carbon dioxide is a heavy, colorless gas that does not have an odor.

carotene (KAR uh teen) or
carotin (KAR uh tihn)
Carotene is a red or yellow color found in plants and animals. Carrots have carotene.

cauliflower (KAW luh flou uhr)
Cauliflower is an annual plant that is eaten as a vegetable.

celery (SEHL uh ree)
Celery is a plant with crisp, long stalks eaten as a vegetable or in salads.

cell (sel)
A cell is the smallest part of all living things.

cereal (SIHR ee uhl)
Cereal is any plant, such as wheat or oats, that produces a grain used for food.

chemist (KEHM ihst)
A chemist is a person who studies simple substances to find out what they are made of, how they act, and how they change.

chlorophyll (KLAWR uh fihl)
Chlorophyll is the green coloring matter made by plants.

chloroplast (KLAWR uh plast)
A chloroplast is a tiny, round package of color found in some plant cells.

chrysanthemum (kruh SAN thuh muhm)
Chrysanthemum is a plant with flowers that bloom in the autumn.

cinnamon (SIHN uh muhn)
Cinnamon is a spice made from the bark of a tropical laurel tree.

coleus (KOH lee uhs)
Coleus is a plant belonging to the mint family, having showy, colorful leaves.

conifer (KOH nuh fuhr)
A conifer is any of a large group of trees and shrubs, most of which are evergreen and bear cones.

conservation (KAHN sir VAY shun)
Conservation is the protection and wise use of natural resources—water, air, soil, minerals, plants, and animals.

cycad (SY kad)
The cycad is a palmlike, cone-bearing plant found in warm areas.

cypress (SY pruhs)
Cypress is an evergreen tree with dark green, overlapping leaves, and hard wood.

dahlia (DAL yuh)
Dahlia is a tall plant having large flowers that bloom in the autumn.

delphinium (del FIHN ee uhm)
Delphinium is a plant that has blue flowers on a tall stalk.

diatom (DY uh tahm)
A diatom is a tiny water plant.

digest (duh JEHST or dy JEHST)
A plant or animal digests food by dissolving it inside itself.

fiber (FY buhr)
A fiber is a long, threadlike piece of a plant.

fungus (FUHNG guhs)
A fungus is a plant without flowers, leaves, or chlorophyll. Two or more such plants are called fungi (FUN jy).

gall (gawl)
A gall is a lump that forms on leaves, stems, or roots of plants where these have been hurt by insects or fungi.

geranium (juh RAY nee uhm)
Geranium is a plant with sweet-smelling leaves and pretty flowers.

ginkgo (GIHNG koh)
Ginkgo is a large tree with leaves shaped like little fans.

gladiolus (GLAD ee OH luhs)
Gladiolus is a plant with long leaves and large, handsome flowers.

heliotrope (HEE lee uh trohp)
Heliotrope is a plant with sweet-smelling flowers that range from light purple to dark blue in color. It is also any plant whose flowers turn to follow the sun.

hepatica (hih PAT uh kuh)
Hepatica is a plant with flowers that bloom in early spring.

herb (urb)
An herb is a plant whose leaves or other parts are used for medicine, seasoning, food, or perfume.

horticulturist
  (hawr tuh KUHL chuhr ihst)
A horticulturist is a person skilled in growing flowers, fruits, vegetables, and other plants.

humus (HYOO muhs)
Humus is a black or dark-brown soil made by the rotting of leaves and other parts of plants.

hyacinth (HY uh sihnth)
The hyacinth is a plant with bunches of little bell-shaped flowers on the ends of long stalks.

Joshua tree (JAHSH u uh tree)
The Joshua tree is a small tree that grows in the desert.

lichen (LY kuhn)
Lichen is fungi and algae plants that are growing together so that they look like one plant. It looks like moss.

macadamia (mak uh DAY mee uh)
Macadamia is a tree or shrub that grows in Hawaii. The nuts are good to eat.

maize (mayz)
Maize is Indian corn.

mineral (MIHN uhr uhl)
A mineral is a substance that is not animal or vegetable.

mistletoe (MIHS uhl toh)
Mistletoe is a plant with small, waxy, white berries and yellow flowers.

oleander (oh le AN duhr)
Oleander is a poisonous evergreen.

orchid (AWR kihd)
Orchid is a plant with beautiful, queerly shaped flowers.

ovule (OH vyool)
The ovule is the part of a plant that develops into a seed.

oxygen (AHK suh juhn)
Oxygen is a gas without color or odor. It is part of the air that you breathe.

papyrus (puh PY ruhs)
Papyrus is a tall water plant once used to make paper.

penicillin (pehn uh SIHL ihn)
Penicillin is a medicine first made from green mold.

penicillium (PEHN uh SIHL ee uhm)
Penicillium is the fungi used to make penicillin.

perennial (puh REHN ee uhl)
A perennial is a plant that lives more than two years.

poinsettia (poyn SEHT ee uh)
Poinsettia is a plant having a small flower surrounded by large red leaves that look like petals.

pollen (PAHL en)
Pollen is a yellowish powder formed in the anthers of flowers. When pollen reaches a flower's ovule, a seed is usually formed.

pollinate (PAHL uh nayt)
To pollinate is to carry pollen from one flower to another.

rhubarb (ROO bahrb)
Rhubarb is a plant whose thick stalks are used for making pies and sauces.

salsify (SAL suh fy)
Salsify is a purple-flowered plant; its roots are eaten as a vegetable.

sassafras (SAS uh fras)
Sassafras is a slender American tree; its bark is used in making medicine, candy, and tea.

seedling (SEED ling)
A seedling is a young plant grown from a seed.

sensitive (SEHN suh tihv)
Anything that responds to an outside force (such as light) is thought of as being sensitive.

sequoia (sih KWOY uh)
Sequoia is a very tall evergreen tree.

sisal (SIHS uhl)
Sisal is a strong fiber used for making rope or twine.

spore (spawr)
A spore is a single cell that comes from a plant and can develop into a new plant.

stigma (STIHG muh)
The stigma is the part of a plant that receives the pollen.

sumac (SOO mak)
Sumac are plants with divided leaves; some are poisonous to the touch.

sycamore (SIHK uh mawr)
Sycamore is a large, common shade tree; its fruit looks like a small, greenish ball.

tamarack (TAM uh rak)
Tamarack is a tree of the pine family with small cones and needles that fall off in the autumn.

tendril (TEHN druhl)
A tendril is the threadlike part of a climbing plant that attaches itself to something and helps support the plant.

thistle (THIHS uhl)
Thistle is a plant that is thickly covered with sharp points.

truffle (TRUHF uhl)
Truffle is a fungus that can be eaten; it grows underground.

tundra (TUHN druh)
The tundra is a great, treeless plain that lies just below the area of ice and snow that surrounds the North Pole.

xanthophyll (ZAN thuh fihl)
Xanthophyll is the yellow color found in autumn leaves.

Illustration Acknowledgments

The publishers of *Childcraft* gratefully acknowledge the courtesy of the following artists, photographers, publishers, agencies, and corporations for illustrations in this volume. When all the illustrations for a sequence of pages are from a single source, the inclusive page numbers are given. In all other instances the page numbers refer to facing pages, which are considered as a single unit or spread. The words "*(left)*," "*(center)*," "*(top)*," "*(bottom)*," and "*(right)*" indicate position on the spread. All illustrations are the exclusive property of the publishers of *Childcraft* unless names are marked with an asterisk (*).

Cover:
(front) Photo by Charles Stone (*)
(back) Standard binding only: illustration by Monica Laimgruber; photo by Ron Church, Tom Stack & Assoc. (*)

Pages   Credits
  1–5: Jean Helmer
  6–23: Gyo Fujikawa
24–25: James Teason
26–27: *(top right)* George Suyeoka; *(bottom)* James Teason
28–29: George Suyeoka
30–31: *(top right)* George Suyeoka; *(bottom)* James Teason
32–39: George Suyeoka
40–41: *(top)* Hermann Eisenbeiss, Photo Researchers (*); *(bottom left)* Jerome Wexler, NAS (*); art: James Teason
42–43: U.S. Dept. of Agriculture (*); art: James Teason
44–45: Harold Hungerford (*)
46–47: Art: Robert Keys; Edward S. Ross (*)
48–49: Jean Helmer
50–51: Irvin L. Oakes, NAS (*)
52–53: *(top left and bottom center)* Sven Samelius (*); *(top right)* Ken Brate, Photo Researchers (*); *(left and right center)* Walter Chandoha (*); *(bottom left)* Russ Kinne, Photo Researchers (*); *(bottom right)* Grant Heilman (*); art: Jean Helmer
54–55: Russ Kinne, Photo Researchers (*)
56–57: *(top left)* Jane Burton, Bruce Coleman, Ltd. (*); *(bottom left)* Edward S. Ross (*); *(top, center and bottom right)* Torkel Korling (*); art: Jean Helmer
58–59: Les Blacklock, Tom Stack & Assoc. (*)
60–61: *(top left and right)* Torkel Korling (*); *(top center)* E. R. Degginger (*); *(bottom left)* G. D. Plage; Bruce Coleman, Ltd. (*); *(bottom center)* Edward S. Ross (*); *(right center)* Harold Hungerford, Tom Stack & Assoc. (*); *(bottom right)* Jack Dermid (*); art: Jean Helmer
62–63: Ron Church (*)
64–65: *(top left and top center)* Ron Church, Tom Stack & Assoc. (*); *(bottom left)* Eileen Tanson, Tom Stack & Assoc. (*); *(center)* Joan E. Rahn (*); *(bottom center)* Walter Dawn (*); *(bottom right)* Carleton Ray, Photo Researchers (*); art: Jean Helmer
66–67: Gale Belinky, Photo Researchers (*)
68–69: *(top left and bottom right)* Noble Proctor, Photo Researchers (*); *(top center and top right)* Les Blacklock, Tom Stack & Assoc. (*); *(bottom left)* Sven Samelius (*); art: Jean Helmer
70–71: Loren McIntyre, Woodfin Camp, Inc. (*)
72–73: *(top left and bottom right)* Edward S. Ross (*); *(top right)* Russ Kinne, Photo Researchers (*); *(bottom left)* G. R. Roberts (*); *(bottom center)* Jacques Jangoux (*); art: Jean Helmer
74–75: Gene Ahrens, Bruce Coleman, Inc. (*)
76–77: *(top left)* R. H. Lynam, Tom Stack & Assoc. (*); *(top center)* Harold Hungerford (*); *(top right)* Paolo Koch, Photo Researchers (*); *(center)* Edward S. Ross (*); *(bottom left)* Andy Bernhaut, Photo Researchers (*); *(bottom center)* Walter Chandoha (*); *(bottom right)* Alan Pitcairn from Grant Heilman (*); art: Jean Helmer
78–79: Steve and Dolores McCutcheon (*)
80–81: *(top left)* Jen and Des Bartlett, Bruce Coleman, Ltd. (*); *(top center)* Russ Kinne, Photo Researchers (*); *(bottom left and center)* Steve and Dolores McCutcheon (*); *(bottom right)* Sven Samelius (*); art: Jean Helmer
82–83: David Muench (*)
84–85: *(top left)* Heinz Schrempp (*); *(top center)* Boyd

Norton (*); (*top right*) Sven Samelius (*); (*bottom left*) V. B. Sheffer, NAS (*); (*center*) Torkel Korling (*); (*bottom right*) Klaus W. Büth, Anthony-Verlag (*); art: Jean Helmer

86–87: Harry McNaught

88–89: (*left*) CHILDCRAFT photos; (*right*) Edward S. Ross (*)

90–91: (*top*) Walter Dawn (*); (*bottom*) CHILDCRAFT photos

92–93: Lou Bory

94–95: Roman Vishniac (*)

96–97: (*top left*) Jane Burton, Bruce Coleman, Ltd. (*); (*top center*) Russ Kinne, Photo Researchers (*); (*bottom left and right*) E. R. Degginger (*)

98–99: (*top left*) Walter Chandoha (*); (*bottom center*) Walter Dawn (*); art: Lou Bory

100–101: (*left*) Carleton Ray, Photo Researchers (*); (*right*) R. H. Lynam, Tom Stack & Assoc. (*)

102–103: (*top left*) Charles Belinky, Photo Researchers (*); (*top center*) Grant Heilman; (*right*) E. R. Degginger (*); (*bottom*) Victor Englebert, Photo Researchers (*)

104–107: Harry McNaught

108–109: Edward S. Ross (*); (*bottom right*) Karl Weidmann

110–111: David Muench (*)

112–113: (*left*) Harold Hungerford (*); (*right*) Edward S. Ross (*)

114–115: (*left*) David Muench (*); (*right*) from *Island Life* by Sherwin Carlquist, © 1965 by Sherwin Carlquist. Reproduced by permission of Doubleday & Company, Inc. (*)

116–117: Harry McNaught

118–121: Betty Fraser

122–123: Hugh Spencer, NAS (*)

124–125: (*top center*) Torkel Korling (*); (*bottom left*) Dorothy M. Compton, NAS (*); art: Betty Fraser

126–127: (*left*) Harold Hungerford (*); (*right*) Betty Fraser

128–129: (*left*) Betty Fraser; (*right*) M. E. Warren (*)

130–131: (*top*) Don Renfro, NAS (*); (*left*) Alvin E. Staffan, NAS (*); (*center*) Edward S. Ross (*); (*right*) Richard Parker, NAS (*); (*bottom*) Larry Moon, Tom Stack & Assoc. (*)

132–133: (*top left*) Jack Dermid, NAS (*); (*bottom left*) Hugh Spencer, NAS (*); art: Betty Fraser

134–135: Grant M. Haist, NAS (*); art: Betty Fraser

136–137: (*left*) John Neel, Tom Stack & Assoc. (*); (*right*) Betty Fraser

138–139: (*bottom left*) Walter Dawn (*); (*right*) Russ Kinne, Photo Researchers (*); art: Betty Fraser

140–141: (*bottom left and top center*) E. R. Degginger (*); (*top left*) Jane Burton, Photo Researchers (*); (*center*) Joan E. Rahn (*); (*bottom center*) Alvin E. Staffan, NAS (*); (*top right*) Edward S. Ross (*); (*bottom right*) C. G. Maxwell, Photo Researchers (*)

142–143: (*left and top left*) Walter Chandoha (*); (*top right*) Veryl Schiebner, Photo Researchers (*); (*bottom center*) Hoppock Assoc. (*); (*bottom right*) Gene Ahrens, Bruce Coleman, Inc. (*)

144–145: Jack Endevelt

146–147: (*top right*) Josephine Von Miklos (*); (*bottom*) C. William Randall

148–149: Wayne Stuart

150–151: CHILDCRAFT photos; art: Wayne Stuart

152–153: Miller Services (*)

154–155: (*left*) Rapho Guillumette (*); (*right*) art: Wayne Stuart

156–161: C. William Randall

162–163: Wayne Stuart

164–167: C. William Randall

168–169: Charles Raymond

170–171: (*left*) Hermann Eisenbeiss (*); (*top*) Gottscho-Shleisner, Inc. (*); (*bottom right*) Longwood Gardens, Kennett Square, Pa. (*)

172–173: (*left*) Frances Bannett, DPI (*); (*top right*)

T. M. McCausland, Bruce Coleman, Inc. (*); (*bottom right*) Ronny Jaques, Photo Researchers (*)

174–175: (*top left*) John Gajda, DPI (*); (*top right*) Van Bucher, Photo Researchers (*); (*bottom*) William McQuitty (*)

176–177: (*top and bottom right*) William McQuitty (*); (*bottom left*) Van Bucher, Photo Researchers (*)

178–195: Robert Keys

196–197: (*left*) Grant Heilman (*); (*right*) Rutherford Platt (*)

198–199: CHILDCRAFT photo; art: Lyle Lamont

200–205: Alex Ebel

206–207: Harold Hungerford (*); art: Alex Ebel

208–209: Alex Ebel

210–211: Edward S. Ross (*); art: Alex Ebel

212–213: Canada Dept. of Agriculture (*); art: Alex Ebel

214–215: Alex Ebel

216–217: CHILDCRAFT photos courtesy Field Museum of Natural History, Chicago

218–219: Robert Keys

220–221: CHILDCRAFT photos

222–223: Norman Weaver

224–225: (*top right*) International Harvester Co. (*); (*bottom right*) Kit and Max Hunn, NAS (*); art: Norman Weaver

226–227: Norman Weaver

228–229: (*left*) Weyerhaeuser Company (*); (*top right*) Grant Heilman (*); (*bottom right*) Fritz Henle, Photo Researchers (*); art: Norman Weaver

230–231: (*top left*) E. R. Degginger (*); (*top right*) Edward S. Ross (*); (*bottom left*) Walter Dawn (*); (*bottom right*) John Moss, Photo Researchers (*)

232–233: CHILDCRAFT photo; art: Norman Weaver

234–235: Charles Stone (*)

236–237: Jack Endevelt

238–239: (*left*) Walter Dawn (*); (*top right*) Edward S. Ross (*); (*bottom right*) Flip Schulke, Black Star (*)

240–241: (*left*) Walter Dawn (*); (*right*) Tuskegee Institute (*)

242–243: (*left*) Peter Larsen (*); (*right*) Walter Dawn (*)

244–245: British Columbia Forest Service (*)

246–247: (*left*) Charles Fiore Nurseries, Inc. (*); (*right*) Miller Services (*)

248–249: (*left*) Three Lions; (*right*) Allied Florist Association of Illinois (*)

250–251: (*left*) Albert Fenn; (*right*) David Muench (*)

252–253: Monica Laimgruber

254–255: Longwood Gardens, Kennett Square, Pa. (*); art: Lilo Fromm

256–257: (*left*) William Stobbs; (*right*) Edward S. Ross (*)

258–259: Miller Services (*); art: Klaus Winter and Helmut Bischoff

260–261: Joy Spurr, Bruce Coleman, Inc. (*); art: Susi Weigel

262–263: (*left*) Pauline Baynes; (*right*) John H. Gerard, NAS (*)

264–265: CHILDCRAFT photo; art: Babs Van Wely

266–267: Lyle Lamont

268–269: Linda Hungerford (*)

270–271: Louis Quitt, NAS (*)

272–273: (*top*) University of Illinois at Urbana (*); (*bottom*) *Chicago Daily News* (*)

274–275: Boyd Norton (*)

276–277: Jack Dermid, Bruce Coleman, Inc. (*)

278–279: Tom Myers, Tom Stack & Assoc. (*)

280–281: Dan Morrill from Vince Kamin (*)

282–283: (*left*) David Muench (*); (*right*) Joan Busta, Tom Stack & Assoc. (*)

284–285: James Milmoe (*)

286–287: (*top left*) John Neel, Tom Stack & Assoc. (*); (*bottom left*) Zaner Miller, Tom Stack & Assoc. (*); (*right*) Joan E. Rahn from Vince Kamin (*)

288–289: (*left*) David Muench (*); (*right*) James Milmoe (*)

290–291: Bill Ratcliffe (*)

Index

This index is an alphabetical list of the important topics covered in this book. It lists topics covered in both words and pictures. By using the index you can find out if a topic is covered and, if so, on what page or pages you will find it. If more than one page is given, the most important page is listed first. Each topic is indexed in a number of ways. Suppose you want to find out something about a tree, but you are not sure of the name. You can find all the tree names listed under the entry **tree name.** Or, if you know the name, you can look under it. For example, **oak** or **white oak.** To help you know what is being referred to, there is often an identifying word in parenthesis after the entry. For example, **acanthus** (plant). If an entry refers *only* to a picture, the word *picture* will come before the page reference. For example, **cannon-ball tree,** *picture, 72.*